Handwriting Without Tears®
Pre-K
Teacher's Guide

**Guide to Multisensory
Lessons and Activities for...**

Handwriting Without Tears®

GET SET FOR SCHOOL

NAME

Coloring, Drawing, Singing, Counting, and
School Readiness

by Jan Z. Olsen, OTR and Emily F. Knapton, OTR/L

Handwriting Without Tears®

Jan Z. Olsen, OTR

8001 MacArthur Blvd
Cabin John, MD 20818
301.263.2700
www.hwtears.com

Authors: Jan Z. Olsen, OTR and Emily F. Knapton, OTR/L
Illustrator: Jan Z. Olsen, OTR
HWT Graphic Designers: Shannon Rutledge, Leah Connor, and Julie Koborg

The Handwriting Without Tears® program and teachers' guides are intuitive and packed with resources and information. Nevertheless, we are constantly developing new ideas and content that make handwriting easier to teach and to learn.

To make this information available to you, we created a password protected section of our website exclusively for users of this teacher's guide. Here you'll find new tips, in-depth information about topics described in this guide, extra practice sheets, other instructional resources, and material you can share with students, parents, and other educators.

Just go to **www.hwtears.com/click** and enter your passcode, **TGGSS8**.

Enjoy the internet resources, and send us any input that you think would be helpful to others: janolsen@hwtears.com.

WELCOME

Welcome to the Get Set for School™ program. The workbook, multisensory products, and music that make up the program have delighted millions of children, parents, and teachers. It has won two of the most prestigious national education awards—The Children's Curriculum Winner from the Association of Educational Publishers and The Teacher's Choice™ Award from *Learning® Magazine*. You'll be amazed at how much your children will enjoy the activities, and you'll be impressed with the progress they make.

The Get Set for School™ program has so many child-friendly, developmentally appropriate materials and activities. Children play, build, sing, color, and learn while developing important skills for kindergarten:

- Language Proficiency
- Social Skills
- Fine and Gross Motor Control

- Color and Shape Awareness
- Letter and Number Recognition
- Counting

The program suits a wide range of children and adapts to their changing needs as they grow. While it has much that's new and different, it still meshes with what good, developmentally-focused teachers have always believed and done with their students. What's unique are the new activities, materials, and songs that develop important skills while still respecting the playful nature of the child. For example:

Children love to sing about and build Mat Man™. They participate eagerly and naturally. They learn how to take turns, follow a sequence, identify body parts, count, and draw.

Children like to handle, sort, and stack the four different Wood Pieces. They learn about big and little lines, big and little curves. Soon they'll use the Wood Pieces to build letters. They learn how to build **B** correctly: first with a big line, and then with two little curves on the right side.

Children naturally learn number concepts as they sing the *Animal Legs* song: "Two legs in the front, two legs in the back, the horse has four legs, I know that." Using the farm animals in the classroom as props, children learn to observe and count legs. There's more than four-legged animals! There are also songs about birds (2 legs), insects (6 legs) and spiders (8 legs) too.

Children who Aim and Scribble in the *Get Set for School* workbook learn how to hold the crayon correctly and progress smoothly to coloring, drawing, and writing letters and numbers.

Pre-k is a joyful time to grow and get ready for school. We developed the activities and products of the Get Set for School™ program to respect the needs and nature of young children, while still preparing them for kindergarten. This book is your guide to those activities and more. It's also a developmental guide with the information about the progression of children's readiness and school skills. We hope that you will enjoy using the Get Set for School™ program with your children, and that you'll be pleased with how well and happily they are playing and learning.

Emily F. Knapton

Emily F. Knapton, OTR/L

Jan Z. Olsen

Jan Z. Olsen, OTR

P.S. As you get further along and see this icon for A Click Away, be sure to visit **www.hwtears.com/click** for more program information and resources.

A B C D E F G H I J K L M N
98 95 87 93 81 80 90 82 84 92 97 79 101 102

Multisensory Lessons...29-59

Music and
Movement...30-33

Wood Pieces, Cards and Mats...34-45

Mat Man™...46-51

Roll-A-Dough Letters™ and
Stamp and See Screen™...52-53

Wet-Dry-Try...54-55

Door Tracing...56-57

Imaginary
Writing...58-59

OPQRSTUVWXYZ

Crayon, Chalk, and Pencil Skills

Why Children (and Teachers) Succeed with HWT

Get Set for School Workbook

EXTRAS

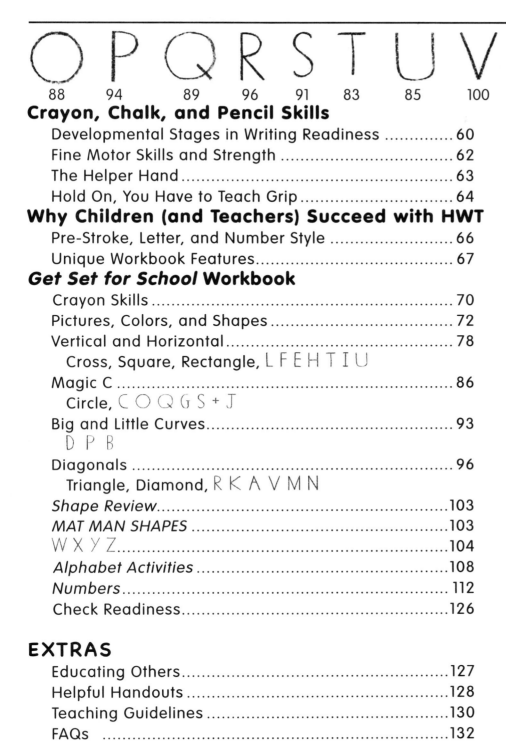

GET SET FOR SCHOOL

NAME

Coloring, Drawing, Singing, Counting, and School Readiness

Need a schedule?
Guidelines are here.

GETTING STARTED
Prepare
ABOUT PRESCHOOLERS

Times are changing. Everybody says that now kindergarten is more like first grade. And what about preschool? Should that be the old kindergarten? We don't think that it should. Preschool should be about preparing children so they can succeed when they start school. They need dressing up, playing outside, riding toys, finger-painting, and finger-plays. They need play to develop socially, emotionally, physically, and mentally. The challenge of this year is to keep it joyful and playful, while still preparing children for the demands of the following year.

Your children are so different from each other and have different strengths. They are also different from how they'll be in just a few months. They come from a variety of home and daycare experiences. They range in age from three to five. With early and late bloomers, with different English language skills, with advantaged and challenged children, you have quite a mix.

As you get to know your students and understand their different learning styles and abilities, this guide will help you bring along those who are missing experiences and skills, while also enhancing the abilities of those who are already ahead. You can develop your students' interest in and abilities to participate, play, and learn. With HWT's multisensory products and the unique activities in this guide, you will be impressed with the progress of all children as they get ready for kindergarten.

EMBRACE YOUR SPACE...

Preschool children learn on all levels. They need floor, table, easel, and outdoor spaces. They're learning as they lie on the floor, sit at a table, stand at an easel, ride a tricycle, and climb up to slide. Much of their active play is self-directed and they can move about as they like. Make sure your space offers a wide range of play and learning places.

However, there are other times during the day when you are reading, demonstrating, or singing. Those teacher-directed times teach not just the story or lesson, but important school behaviors for looking and listening. Help children do well by ensuring they can easily see and hear you. When they face you, it is easier for them to pay attention and learn. This is so simple, but so helpful in developing their skills.

For Preschool Children

What about your furniture? Be sure that you have enough variety in table and chair sizes that you can position your students well for table activities. You'll want them to have their feet on the floor and the table at a good height for all table activities. Because children grow and range in size, you'll do best with a variety of sizes. Be willing to move your furniture to suit your day and your activities. Children can easily slide or lift chairs, and this is a good cooperative, physical, and spatial activity.

For Demonstrations

Mat Man™
Demonstrate on the floor how to build Mat Man. Use Wood Pieces, Mat, and the pattern on page 50.

Pre-K Wall Cards
Display the alphabet above the board to help children remember letters.

Name Cards
Give each child a place in the room. Model names in capitals and title case.

For Multisensory Readiness

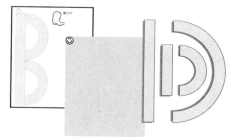

Get Set for School Sing Along CD
Use the CD to make learning readiness skills fun and memorable.

Wood Pieces Set, Capital Letter Cards & Mat
Use these readiness materials to develop skills in a playful but carefully structured way. The Mat and Cards use a ☺ as an orientation icon for the Wood Pieces.

Roll-A-Dough Letters™ & Stamp and See Screen™
Exploring letters has never been so fun.

Slate & Blackboard with Double Lines
Use the Slate to teach capitals and numbers. Use the Blackboard with Double Lines to teach children their names.

For the Children

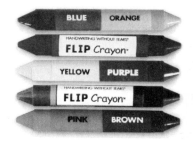

Magic C Bunny
Make the puppet your teaching assistant. Your students can use him too.

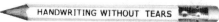

Get Set for School Workbook
This engaging and fun workbook helps children build good foundation habits. It develops children's coloring, drawing, and beginning writing skills.

FLIP Crayons™
Flip Crayons help children develop hand coordination and fine motor skills.

Pencils for Little Hands
Use golf-size pencils with children. Let them write with pencils that fit their hands.

THE PRESCHOOL CHILD AND THE PRE-K YEAR
Your Developmentally Based Pre-K Program

Across the nation, there are thousands of excellent preschools—places where children play and learn joyfully. We are great admirers of preschool teachers and their programs. We admire how they help children develop physically, socially, and mentally. We see how well students develop strength, stamina, and other skills through active outdoor and indoor play. They develop self-help skills as they don jackets, wash hands, and set out snacks. They learn social skills. They share, take turns, wait, listen, participate, and cooperate. Day by day, they master new words, shapes, letters, numbers, rhymes, songs, and stories.

Adding the Get Set For School™ Curriculum

The Get Set for School curriculum fits easily into the daily preschool routine. As teachers become familiar with the program, they gradually incorporate new activities, choosing activities that suit their children's readiness level. Here's how:

Building

You're already using sturdy wood blocks because they invite children to a world of imagination and self-directed play where they are active, moving, turning, and placing objects.

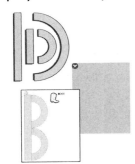

ADD THE WOOD PIECES SET
Included are Wood Pieces in the four basic shapes used to build capital letters:
8 big lines, 6 little lines, 6 big curves, 6 little curves

As children polish, sort, and stack, they learn the names of the Wood Pieces. Using Wood Pieces in teacher-directed play, children learn size, shape, and position concepts. When they're ready for letters, they use the Wood Piece language and concepts to build letters. For example, we make letter **B:** big line, little curve, little curve.

Music, Circle Time, and Fingerplays

You sing to them and with them. There are songs for starting, saying good-bye, and picking up toys. Children love to participate and play simple instruments. For some, it is music that unlocks language.

ADD THE *GET SET FOR SCHOOL SING ALONG* CD.
At first, just play the CD during free play time until you and the children become familiar with the tunes and words. You'll soon find favorite songs and fingerplays to use during circle time and through the day.

Playing With Dough

Children like to play with dough. All that pinching, squeezing, rolling, and pressing helps develop small muscles in their hands. They feel and see size and shape differences.

ADD ROLL-A-DOUGH LETTERS™
They can roll balls into snakes, and use snakes to make letters. Letter and number cards model a dough letter. Children simply roll out the dough and place it on the card. Build **A** by rolling 2 big lines and 1 little line.

Drawing and Painting

Drawing is the trace of movement. Through play with finger paint, chalk, and crayons, children discover the relationship between how they move and the marks they make. They begin to make shapes, and to draw simple people and things: a sun, a tree, etc.

ADD MAT MAN™

He's a very simple man, made of Wood Pieces and a blue Mat. Building him with the teacher helps children learn spatial and drawing concepts. He gives them a sense of body part placement so they can draw him and other people. He helps children have fun learning.

Colors and Coloring

Children know, or soon will know, the primary and secondary colors. They can find, match, and name them. You give them opportunities to color on the floor, on the table, or at the easel. You provide small bits of colored chalk or crayon, knowing that small pieces naturally promote a good grip and finger strength.

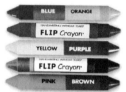

ADD *PICK UP A CRAYON* song and FLIP CRAYONS™

Use the song to teach your children how to place their fingers and hold the crayon correctly. That's the best start for handwriting skills because a good crayon grip leads to a good pencil grip. The Flip Crayons delight children and encourage them to move their fingers to flip the crayon to a new color.

Language and Letters

You read to, talk to, and sing with children. The classrooms have words and the alphabet on display. Children's names are on cubbies and charts. They have a rich language and letter environment.

ADD LETTER PLAY ACTIVITIES and THE *GET SET FOR SCHOOL* WORKBOOK

Show children how to build letters with the Wood Pieces and how to write letters on the Slate with Wet–Dry–Try. Then use the workbook to teach letter strokes and how writing letters correctly, starting at the top and making them in the correct sequence.

Counting and Numbers

Children can count out loud. You have taught them to notice the number of fingers on your hand, legs on a dog, and wheels on a car. You have taught them one-to-one correspondence.

ADD THE *GET SET FOR SCHOOL SING ALONG* CD AND THE SLATE CHALKBOARD

At first, children learn to count on their own bodies. Songs such as *Count on Me*, *Five Fingers Play*, and *Toe Song* teach an awareness of numbers. Use the Wet–Dry–Try activity with the Slate to teach students how to write numbers 1 through 10 correctly and without reversals.

Social and Emotional Readiness

You guide them as they learn to share, care for themselves, respect others, and follow routines. You take them as they are and help them develop important behaviors for school.

ADD ANY ACTIVITY

Have a child sort Wood Pieces with two other children. The child is skilled at sorting, but needs practice cooperating. Pick and choose activities, not just for their stated purpose, but for how they foster social skills. During the day and during the year, you're helping children develop in many ways.

The Role of Readiness in Early Literacy and Handwriting
INFORMAL VS FORMAL HANDWRITING INSTRUCTION

This curriculum is not about formal handwriting instruction. Preschoolers simply are not ready for either formal paper-pencil lessons or for kindergarten style worksheets. Preschoolers need an informal readiness program that suits their developmental needs and abilities. Here's the difference between informal handwriting readiness and formal instruction:

INFORMAL

Informal Handwriting Readiness
Structured, teacher selected activities

When
Preschool and kindergarten

Readiness Materials
Get Set for School Sing Along CD, Wood Pieces Set, Mat, Slate, Roll-A-Dough Letters™, Stamp and See Screen™ (Used for instruction)

Writing Materials
Get Set for School workbook (a crayon book)
Unlined paper, paper strips for Name
Chalk, crayon

Pre-handwriting skills
Attention
Behavior
Language
Imitation
Stop/start
Fine motor

FORMAL

Formal Handwriting Instruction
Structured, teacher directed lessons

When
Kindergarten

Readiness Materials
Wood Pieces, Mat, Slate
(Used before paper/pencil instruction)

Writing Materials
Letters and Numbers for Me workbook
(a pencil book)
Lined paper
Chalk, crayon, pencil

Handwriting
How to hold a pencil correctly
Form capitals, lowercase letters, and numbers
Write simple words and sentences
Develop top-to-bottom, left-to-right orientation
for reading/writing

The informal handwriting program prepares children to hold a crayon, color and draw, and imitate a few capitals and numbers. Beginning writing skills prepare a child to do well in a formal handwriting program.

Informal or Formal?
All young children should participate in readiness because the activities promote effective learning. Readiness activities appeal to the children's varied learning styles. The hands-on letter play also offers social and motor skills benefits. This prepares children for formal handwriting instruction. Even in kindergarten, formal instruction should not begin until children can demonstrate the following:

1. Hand dominance
2. Knowledge of simple size and shape concepts for big line/little line, big curve/little curve
3. Ability to hold a crayon with the fingers placed correctly
4. Satisfactory level of attention, cognitive skills, and cooperation
5. Imitation of a vertical line, horizontal line, circle, and cross

Three Levels of Readiness

Readiness levels are based on skill mastery. Children move from one level to another at different ages. Children involved in readiness activities range in age from 3 to 6 years.

Readiness Level 1—Preparing Young Children

This early level invites everyone's participation. Play the *Get Set for School Sing Along* CD in the background so that you and the children become familiar with the songs and activities. Soon they'll be singing the ABCs, counting legs on animals, and making Mat Man™. They'll use Wood Pieces to build letters on Letter Cards and Mats. The social interaction and language aspects of these activities make them worthwhile for children at all levels.

Readiness Level 2—Hands-On Letter Play

This level focuses on developing fine motor skills and beginning letter skills. Show children how to hold and use a crayon to aim and scribble, and to color pictures and shapes in the *Get Set for School* workbook. At the same time, they'll continue to develop beginning letter skills through play. They'll roll out dough snakes to make Roll-A-Dough Letters™. They'll stamp and trace letters with the Stamp and See Screen™.

Readiness Level 3—Crayon Skills

Now children begin writing. Continue to use the *Crayon Song* to be sure they're holding the crayon correctly. Continually demonstrate and supervise. Your modeling is so important at this stage. Use the Slate, Wet–Dry–Try activity just before you introduce the crayon stroke letters in the *Get Set for School* workbook. The Wet–Dry–Try activity directly teaches correct orientation and formation habits. Students will learn how to make the letters before they write. Show children how to write their names.

DEVELOPMENTAL TEACHING ORDER

The readiness activities have prepared children for success with capital letters. Now, they're ready to begin coloring, tracing lines, making shapes, and writing letters and numbers in *Get Set for School*.

Crayon Skills

Begin with Crayon Skills

The Aim and Scribble pages are unique. Use these pages when teaching beginning crayon skills: picking up, holding, aiming/placing, and moving the crayon. It's so nice for beginners to just land on a star or firefly and make it shine by wiggling and scribbling. Children have fun learning basic crayon skills with these pictures.

Fill In Coloring—Colors, Pictures, and Shapes

Fill-in coloring is next. Children now learn to move the crayon more deliberately. The pictures and shapes encourage them to stay within a certain area and use back and forth, up and down, or side-to-side strokes. The pictures and shapes are easy to color. They have bold outlines and no tiny details or overlapping parts. When using these pages, the teacher helps children learn the names of all the pictures, colors, and shapes. Some are new! Children begin to think of shapes as they relate to objects or pictures. Fill-in coloring will continue throughout the book.

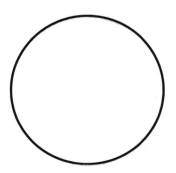

Benefits of Coloring

It's a joy watching children color because they have fun and freedom to be creative. Developmentally, children will color broadly over an illustration. As their skills develop, their movements will progress smaller, more refined strokes. Because coloring is such a common activity, we forget the great benefits it has for developing coordination, grip, and strength. By observing how children color, you can determine their handwriting readiness with the following skills:

- Attention
- Crayon Grip
- Control
- Posture/Strength/Endurance
- Use of the Helping Hand

Help children color:

1. Choose easy to color, appealing illustrations.
2. Help children hold the crayon.
   (See page 64-65 for teaching crayon grip.)
3. Demonstrate coloring on a separate page.
   - Side-to-side (horizontal) strokes
   - Up-and-down vertical strokes
   - Little circular motions
   - Staying in the lines or following the direction of the lines
4. Encourage children to draw on the illustrations.

Generally, the shape of the illustration will determine which stroke a child uses. See the crayon stroke pattern on the cow above. If a child is unable to organize his/her stroke to accommodate the shape of the illustration, encourage the child to color up/down because that is easiest.

Pre-Strokes, Letters, and Numbers

Vertical and Horizontal

cross   L   F   square   E   F   rectangle   H T U I

Magic C

C O   circle   Q G S   J

Big and Little Curves

D P B

Diagonals

R K A   triangle   diamond   V M N

More Diagonals   Numbers

W X Y Z   1 2 3 4 5 6 7 8 9

ABOUT FREE WRITING

Preschool teachers often ask for our opinion about free writing.

Free writing is letting children write without specific instruction. In the preschool environment, it's not uncommon to see children free writing at centers or on their papers. At this age, they typically will use it during imaginary play to act grown up. It's innocent curiosity.

We consider two types of free writing. One is directly tied to what some consider to be handwriting instruction (see Sample 1). The other is tied to children curiously forming letters and numbers from what is referred to as Environmental Print (see Sample 2).

Sample 1 - Using free writing to teach children handwriting is trouble. For handwriting, it isn't appropriate to just pass out worksheets for practice. Children who are left to their own resources to figure out writing letters, become self-taught writers. Their completed letters may look okay, but the letters often are formed with inconsistent or bad habits. These children may survive the kindergarten work load, but fall apart when writing demands increase. These children often need remediation simply because they weren't taught properly.

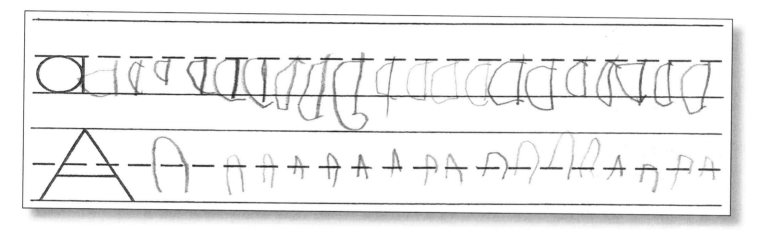

Sample 2 - Environmental printing is fine, but it needs to be followed by explicit instruction of how to write the letters. Once taught, children must stick consistently to the correct habit. Environmental printing won't lead to any ingrained bad habits as long as you follow up with explicit instruction.

STAGES OF LEARNING

Now that you understand printing skills and the role you play in developing handwriting, you will better understand the stages of learning. Children typically learn in a developmental order. Too often, we find ourselves in such a hurry that we rush ahead. Children learn to write correctly and easily when instructions follow these developmentally based stages. You may need to review some of the pre-instructional readiness concepts below before advancing to the more formal instructional steps that follow:

Pre-Instructional Readiness (Pre-K and Kindergarten)

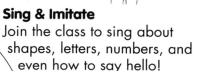

Sing & Imitate
Join the class to sing about shapes, letters, numbers, and even how to say hello!

Make Mat Man™
Take turns. Learn body parts and how to draw with Mat Man.

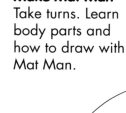

Build Letters
Know how to pick and place Wood Pieces to build letters.
(D = one big line + one big curve)

Trace on a Slate
Make capitals and numbers on a reversal-proof slate! Do it with multisensory Wet–Dry–Try.

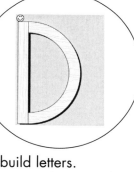

Share, Play, Socialize
Participate, take turns, and communicate with materials, music, and teacher modeling.

Color and Write
Practice in a child friendly workbook, with pictures and models that promote good habits.

Instructional Stages Ahead

When the pre-instructional readiness skills have been established, handwriting instruction proceeds in three stages (Imitation, Copying, and Independent Writing). Multisensory activities can enhance learning in every stage.

Stage 1 – Imitation

The child watches as the teacher writes and then imitates the teacher.

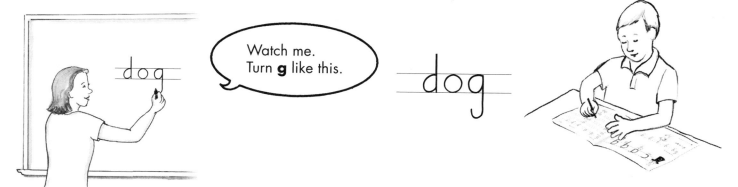

See the motions as the teacher writes step-by-step.

Hear the directions.

See the model.

Write **dog**.

Stage 2 – Copying

The child looks at the completed model of a letter, word, or sentence and copies it, trying to match the model.

See the model.

Write **dog**.

Stage 3 – Independent Writing

The child writes unassisted, without a demonstration or a model.

Write **dog**.

THE INTENT TO PREVENT

Good handwriting skills result from thoughtful attention and instruction. Students require deliberate instruction to develop good habits and overcome bad ones. The earlier we instill good habits, the better the result. What you teach in preschool affects later handwriting development.

With this guide and HWT materials, you will be prepared to help preschoolers become natural and automatic writers. You'll find that their abilities vary. Regardless of where they start, you can help them develop good skills. In later grades, teachers are required to do two things; teach and correct (see below). By starting early, you can instill good habits, thus minimizing the need for correction or remediation.

Teach	**Fix**
How to hold the pencil correctly	Awkward pencil grips

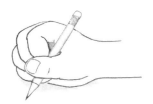

Letters/numbers that face the right way	Reversals

Letters/numbers that start at the top	Starting at the bottom

Letters/numbers that are formed correctly and consistently	Incorrect letter/number

PRINTING SKILLS FOR SPEED AND LEGIBILITY

When children begin formal handwriting instruction, we want them to write with speed and neatness while thinking about the content of their work. In preschool, our priority is on Memory, Orientation, Start, and Sequence. Even as they become familiar with these skills, children won't master them fully until formal handwriting instruction begins.

Would you like to know the secret of developing speed and legibility? Some people think it's practice, practice, practice that promotes speed. But practicing letters over and over actually makes letters progressively messier. Some think that trying hard is what makes printing neat. But trying hard won't work unless children have been taught properly.

The secret to achieving speed and legibility is following the simple strategies in the HWT workbooks, guides, and multisensory products. The HWT program develops eight key skills:

Memory	Identify letters and numbers quickly from a random list.
	Visualize a letter or number quickly without seeing it.
Orientation	Print all letters and numbers without reversals.
Placement	Follow lines and place letters and numbers correctly on the baseline.
Size	Write an appropriate size for grade level.
	Make letters a consistent size.
Start	Start all letters and numbers at the top (except **d** and **e**).
Sequence	Make the letter parts in the correct order and direction.
	Make the letter parts the same correct way every time.
Control	Print the letter parts neatly–no gaps, overlaps, or extra tracings.
	Keep curved parts curved, straight parts straight, pointed parts pointed, etc.
Spacing	Keep letters in words close.
	Leave space between words in sentences.

It is clear that each of these skills is important. We start to develop these skills in preschool. Children who immediately know their letters or numbers and which way they face (Memory and Orientation) don't have to stop and think. They can write quickly. Children who make their letters sit correctly on the baseline and who make them a consistent size (Placement and Size) produce neat papers. Children who always start in the right place, and make the strokes the same way every time (Start and Sequence) are able to write quickly and neatly without thinking. (Control) will come naturally as children master the above skills. (Spacing) develops from good instruction and from using the worksheets and workbooks that provide enough room to write.

Speed and Neatness

Music teachers know about speed. It's the last thing they teach. First come the notes, rhythm, fingering or bowing, and finally, practice to reach an automatic, natural level. Then pick up the tempo! It's the same with handwriting. Take a lesson from a music teacher! Work on everything else and speed will come. Children who use poor habits are doomed to be slow or sloppy. Children with good habits can be both fast and neat. That's where we are heading.

SCOPE AND SEQUENCE OF PRINTING

The Scope and Sequence of Printing defines the content and order of printing instruction. The skills needed for printing develop as early as preschool. Although we do not teach printing formally at the preschool level, we can informally create an environment and encourage activities to help students develop good habits they will need later. The secret is teaching skills in a way that makes learning natural and fun.

Description

Type of Instruction

Informal/Structured: A variety of activities address the broad range of letter and school readiness skills.
Formal/Structured: Teacher directed activities are presented in a more precise order with specific objectives.

Handwriting Sequence

Pre-Strokes: These are beginning marks that are made randomly or deliberately.
Shapes: Shapes often are introduced before letters and are a foundation for letter formation skills.
Capitals/Numbers: These use simple shapes and strokes. They have the same size, start, and position.
Lowercase Letters: These are tall, small, and descending symbols with more complex strokes, sizes, starts, and positions.

Stages of Learning

Pre-Instruction Readiness: This is attention, behavior, language, and fine motor skills for beginning writing.

Stage 1: Imitating the Teacher: This is watching someone form a letter first, and then writing the letter.
Stage 2: Copying Printed Models: This is looking at a letter and then writing the letter.
Stage 3: Independent Writing: This is writing without watching someone or even seeing a letter.

Physical Approach

Crayon Use: Crayons prepare children for using pencils. Using small crayons encourages proper grip.
Pencil Use: Proper pencil use is necessary for good handwriting. In kindergarten, children transfer their crayon grip to pencils.
Posture: Good sitting posture promotes good handwriting. This is taught in kindergarten.
Paper Placement: When children are writing sentences and paragraphs, they're ready to angle the paper so they can move the writing hand easily across the page.

Printing Skills

Primary Skills
    Memory: Remember and write dictated letters and numbers.
    Orientation: Face letters and numbers in the correct direction.
    Start: Begin each letter or number correctly.
    Sequence: Make the letter strokes in the correct order.
Secondary Skills
    Placement: Place letters and numbers on the baseline.
    Size: Write in a consistent, grade appropriate size.
    Spacing: Place letters in words closely, putting space between words.
    Control: Focus on neatness and proportion.

Functional Writing

Letters/Numbers
Words
Sentences
Paragraphs
Writing in All Subjects

SCOPE AND SEQUENCE OF PRINTING

	PK	K	1	2
Type of Instruction				
Informal/Structured	X			
Formal/Structured		X	X	X
Handwriting Sequence				
Pre-Strokes	X			
Shapes	X			
Capitals/Numbers	X	X	X	X
Lowercase Letters	*See note below	X	X	X
Stages of Learning				
Pre-Instruction Readiness	X	X		
Stage 1: Imitating the Teacher	X	X	X	X
Stage 2: Copying Printed Models		X	X	X
Stage 3: Independent Writing		X	X	X
Physical Approach				
Crayon Use	X	X		
Pencil Use		X	X	X
Posture		X	X	X
Paper Placement		X	X	X
Printing Skills				
Primary Skills				
Memory	X	X	X	X
Orientation	X	X	X	X
Start	X	X	X	X
Sequence	X	X	X	X
Secondary Skills				
Placement		X	X	X
Size		X	X	X
Spacing		X	X	X
Control		X Emerging	X	X
Functional Writing				
Letters/Numbers	X Capitals/Numbers	X	X	
Words		X Short	X Short	X Long
Sentences		X Short	X Short	X Long
Paragraphs			X Short	X Long
Writing in All Subjects		X	X	X

*Children in preschool are taught lowercase letter recognition – but not writing. They may be taught the lowercase letters in their names.

Get Set For School™ Readiness

Many of your preschoolers may have been exposed to a variety of readiness skills. Many have not. The next section of this guide is dedicated to getting your preschoolers off to the best start. This information is valuable to you because your students' skills vary. Some need social skills and some need motor skills.

EASEL ART AND FINE MOTOR

An Easel to Share

Standing up and working against gravity helps build strength in the shoulders and arms. An easel is ideal for wrist position too. You may want to consider turning an old bi-fold door into a big community easel. In preschool and kindergarten, we suggest putting less experienced children by the more experienced. Children learn through imitation. Because it's a communal picture, there is no concern about the final product. It's as appealing as graffiti. Place small baskets of FLIP Crayons™ around the easel. Let children doodle freely.

Fine Motor Skills

Many of the preschool activities incorporate fine motor experiences. Often, preschoolers (especially boys) need some additional fine motor support. Consider using the *Get Set For School Sing Along* CD, Tracks 10 and 16, for finger play activities. We have included a few of our favorite suggested activities for improving and practicing fine motor skills. For more tips and ideas you can send home to parents, visit, **www.hwtears.com/click**.

- Do finger–plays. Find them in a book at the library.
- Cut pictures out of newspapers or magazines. Take a large black marker and draw a line around the picture to give a guideline.
- Have children put together small beads, Legos®, Tinker Toys®, Lincoln Logs®, etc.
- Knead dough or clay. Build objects with them.
- Hide small objects in the dough and have children find them.
- Play peg board games.
- Play with any toys that require moving or placing little pieces.
- Let children squirt water bottles outdoors on the sidewalk.
- Squeeze a kitchen baster to move a cotton ball with air. Have a race on the table.
- Finger paint on a paper plate with Jell-O® or cocoa.
- Use small marshmallows and toothpicks to form letters.
- String popcorn, buttons, beads to make necklaces.

SHAKE HANDS WITH ME

This activity teaches right/left discrimination and an important social skill: greeting others.

Preparation

Each day, choose a different sensory stimulus (touch, scent, liquid, solid, visual, auditory).
Here are a few suggestions:
- Lotion, rubber stamp, flavoring, water in a bowl, and so forth

Directions

1. Shake hands with each child. Smile, make eye contact, and say, "Hello."
2. Say, "This is your right hand. I'm going to do something to your right hand."
   Lotion—Put a dab on the right thumb and index finger. "Rub your fingers together."
   Rubber Stamp—Stamp the right hand. "Look at your right hand now."
   Flavoring—Dab some flavoring (e.g. peppermint) on the right index finger. "Smell that peppermint."
3. Direct students to raise their right hands and say with you:
   - "This is my right hand."
   - "I shake hands with my right hand."

Skills Developed

- Social Skills—For meeting and greeting
- Right/Left Discrimination—Only the right hand is for shaking
- Directionality—A sense of directionality with the body

Shake Hands with a Friend

Another way to teach right/left discrimination is to have children shake hands with a friend. This activity is a wonderful way to encourage socialization and acceptance in the classroom. Try the following activity:
1. Use the *Get Set for School Sing Along* CD, Track 7.
2. Have children stand in pairs.
3. Play the CD. Begin by just singing, then shake hands and say "hi" to each other.
4. Have the children shake hands while singing the song.

Hello Song

Little kids can wave bye, bye
But only big kids know
How to stand perfectly still
And say, "Hello"

Give 'em your right hand
Look 'em in the eye
Put a smile on your face
Then you say, "Hi"
Repeat 1X

"It's nice to meet you
How do you do?"
They'll be so happy
To be meeting you
Greetings are a way to say
"I hope you have a wonderful day"

Give 'em your right hand
Look 'em in the eye
Put a smile on your face
Then you say, "Hi"
Repeat 1X

I'm a big kid and I know
To use my right hand when I say hello
To put my right hand for you to take
We meet each other and we shake
Shake, shake, So

Give 'em your right hand
Look 'em in the eye
Put a smile on your face
Then you say, "Hi"
Repeat 3X

LEARNING THE TOP!

English is a top-to-bottom, left-to-right language. That's the way we read and write. The top-to-bottom habit is the key to printing quickly and neatly. Children who start letters at the top don't have to think about making letters. They can print automatically and quickly without becoming sloppy. Starting at the bottom causes difficulty because it is impossible to write quickly without becoming sloppy. This demonstration proves the importance of starting at the top. Try it!

Make 5 lines down. Make 5 lines, alternating down/up.   Now do it again, quickly.

↓ | | | | | ↓↑ | | | | | ↓ | | | | | ↓↑ (| \ | |
slow   slow   fast   fast

By starting at the top, you can be both fast and neat. Children who start letters at the bottom often are slow or sloppy.

Sing About It – *Where Do You Start Your Letters?*

In this guide, you'll learn how to develop good habits. Start by teaching this fun song. You know the tune: *If You're Happy and You Know It*. The lyrics for *Where Do You Start Your Letters?* are below. A slower version is available on our *Get Set for School Sing Along* CD, Track 1. It's perfect for preschoolers. Children will have great fun singing and dancing while learning the difference between top, bottom, and middle. Be sure to also try our rock-n-roll version (it includes numbers too). You can find it on our *Rock, Rap, Tap & Learn* CD, Track 2.

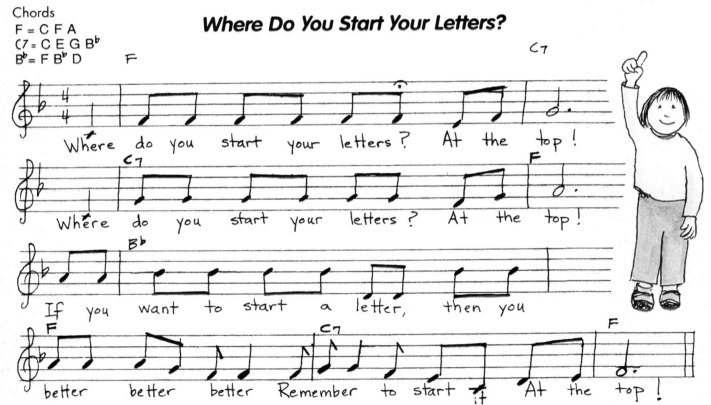

Where Do You Start Your Letters?

Chords
F = C F A
C7 = C E G B♭
B♭ = F B♭ D

Where do you start your letters? At the top!
Where do you start your letters? At the top!
If you want to start a letter, then you
better better better Remember to start it At the top!

Use this song when you're teaching or reviewing PRINTED CAPITALS.

Tune: *If You're Happy and You Know It*

BASIC STROKES: SIGN IN PLEASE!

Because some letters are easier to form than others, in pre-k and kindergarten we teach pre-strokes to children based on developmental principles. *Studies show that children gradually develop the ability to copy forms in a very predictable order as shown below:

* Gessell, Arnold, and others. *The First Years of Life.* New York: Harper and Row. 1940.

Alphabet Sign-In

This activity is fun and develops many important skills. Preschoolers can have fun by signing in alphabetically.

Preparation

1. Prepare blackboard with a wide stop line near the bottom. (A blackboard is best, but you can use a white board.)
2. Use 1" pieces of chalk to encourage correct grip.

Directions

1. Teacher prints **A**.
   - Write **A** up high, but within children's reach.
   - Teach **A** and each letter that follows as you write.
   - Use consistent words as you demonstrate: **A** = big line, big line, and little line.
2. Teacher asks, "Whose name begins with **A**? Adam!"
3. Adam comes to the board and you introduce him, saying:
   "This is…" (children say "Adam").
   "Adam starts with…" (children say **A**).
   "In Adam's name, the **A** makes the sound…" (children make the **A** sound).
4. Adam signs in by making a big line down from **A**. He stops on the line.
5. Repeat this exercise with each letter. Children sign in alphabetically.

Skills Developed

- Top-to-bottom letter formation
- Stopping on a line
- Names of capital letters and of classmates
- Letter sounds using classmates' names
- Big line, little line, big curve, little curve to understand the parts of each capital letter
- Alphabetical order
- Left-to-right sequencing
- Social skills including following directions, cooperating, listening, taking turns, interacting in groups
- Chalk and pencil grip
- Number concepts including counting and comparing by counting the lines for each letter.

Variation

You can change how children sign in to teach other skills:
- Horizontal line skills: underline letter from left to right
- Circle skills: circle the letter by starting at the top with a **C** stroke

CAPITALIZING ON THE CAPITALS

Teachers agree that capitals are easier, and that's where we begin. When children learn to write their capitals, they develop a strong foundation for printing. They learn important handwriting rules (such as a top-to-bottom, left-to-right habit), proper letter formation, and solid visual memory for capital letters.

Children who learn capitals first also learn the following:
- Start letters at the top.
- Use the correct stroke sequence to form letters.
- Orient letters and numbers correctly—no reversals!

Learning capitals first makes learning lowercase letters a breeze. Think about it: **c o s v w x y z** are the same as capitals; **j k t p** and **u** also are similar to their capital partners. If we teach capitals correctly, we have already prepared children for nearly half of the lowercase alphabet.

Why Are Capitals Easier Than Lowercase Letters?

Capital letters are easy
- All start at the top.
- All are the same height.
- All occupy the same vertical space.
- All are easy to recognize and identify (compare **A B D G P Q** with **a b d g p q**.)
- Capitals are big, bold, and familiar.

Lowercase letters are more difficult
- Lowercase letters start in four different places. (**a b e f**)
- Lowercase letters are not the same size. Fourteen letters are half the size of capitals. Twelve are the same size as capitals.
- Lowercase letters occupy three different vertical positions—small, tall, descending.
- Lowercase letters are more difficult to recognize because of subtle differences (**a b d g p q**).

Let's do the math
You can see at a glance that capitals are easier for children. Students have fewer chances to make mistakes when they write capital letters. They aim the pencil at the top and get it right. With lowercase, there are many more variables.

When teaching handwriting, teach capitals first. You will save yourself time, make life easier for children, and get better handwriting results.

CAPITAL AND LOWERCASE LETTER ANALYSIS		
	Capitals	**Lowercase**
Start	1	4
Size	1	2
Position	1	3
Appearance	• Familiar • Distinctive A B D G P Q	• Many similar • Easy to confuse a b d g p q

A PRE-PENCIL, PRE-PAPER START

Children who use HWT in preschool benefit from unique pre-pencil and paper lessons for learning capital letters. In preschool and kindergarten, children use the Wood Pieces Set for Capital Letters to learn letter formation. We give these pieces unique names to teach capitals with consistency.

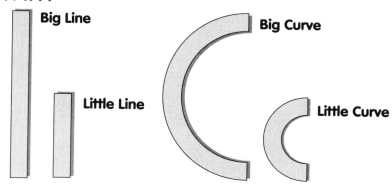

Big Line

Little Line

Big Curve

Little Curve

Children make letters with the Capital Letter Cards, Mat, and Slate. All have a smiley face in the top left corner. These tools help students form each letter correctly, systematically, and without reversals.

 The Secret of the Smile

The smiley face shows that the letter is right side up and promotes good top-to-bottom, left-to-right habits.

Capital Letter Card

Mat

Slate

Teach preschoolers capital letter language (big line, little line, big curve, little curve) by modeling letters. Say each stroke as you demonstrate the letter.

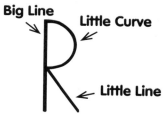

Big Line **Little Curve**

Little Line

In addition to using our Capital Letter Cards, Mat, and Slate, children can have fun rolling and stamping letters too. Our Roll-A-Dough Letters™ and Stamp and See Screen™ activities are the perfect center-based activities for the preschool environment.

Roll-A-Dough Letters™

Tray Cards for Roll-A-Dough fit Stamp and See Screen™

Stamp and See Screen™

TRACING SECRETS

Tracing letters has always been popular. Unlike standard dotted tracing, we recommend tracing a gray crayon stroke. A solid line gives children a sense of letter completeness. The color gray is a good option because it disappears when a child traces over it. Tracing is good only when it is accompanied by adult demonstration.

If you want to do some tracing with preschoolers:

- Use a highlighter pen or gray crayon to make letters.

- Stay away from dots! Dots are visually confusing and some children will even take the time to connect one dot to the next.

- Clearly indicate (see arrow on the right above **A**) where the child should start the stroke. We use this special icon in the *Get Set for School* workbook. When making your own tracing activities, a tiny star or small dot will do.

- Provide tracing tips and activities for children to use at home. Often, children get their first experiences with tracing from their parents.

A Tracing Activity - HWT Capital and Number Practice Strips

When teaching children their names, phone numbers, and simple words, consider using a gray crayon and our Capital and Number Practice Strips. Phone numbers are a great place to start.

Preparation
1. Gather one Capital and Number Practice Strip.
2. Have a gray crayon, other colored crayons, and strips available.

Directions
1. Adult uses the gray crayon to model one number at a time on the strip.
2. Child chooses a different color to trace the adult's model.

Skills Developed
- Letter/number recognition
- Letter/number formation
- Life skills (name, phone number)
- Word recognition

Tips
- Have children practice saying the numbers out loud.
- Go on a hunt for words written with only capitals. Bring the list back to class and write them on the strips for children to trace.

TEACHING SHAPES
Build, Color, Trace, Sing, and Draw Shapes

Learning shapes doesn't have to be boring. Use these fun, easy ideas for teaching shapes.

Build Shapes with Wood Pieces

See this guide: pages 34-45 to learn about Wood Pieces.

Directions

1. Demonstrate making shapes on the floor.
   - Circles = 2 big curves or 2 little curves
   - Crosses = 2 big lines or 2 little lines
   - Squares = 4 big lines or 4 little lines
   - Triangles = 3 big lines or 3 little lines
   - Rectangle = 2 big lines and 2 little lines
2. Ask children to hand you the pieces as you build the shapes.
3. Always start the circles with a **C**.
4. Leave your models on the floor for children to copy.

Color Shapes in the workbook

See this guide: pages 72-76 for specific instructions.

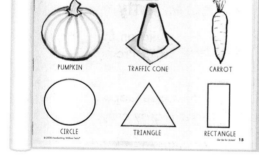

Directions

1. Teach the name of the shape.
2. Finger trace the shapes.
3. Help the children choose the right color crayon.
4. Show children how to move the crayon to follow the shapes.

Trace Shapes in the workbook

See this guide pages: 79, 80, 82, 99, 103 for specific instructions.

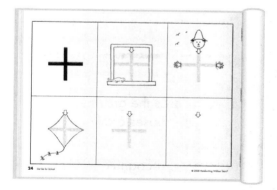

Directions

1. Teach these pages as they arise in the workbook.
2. Teach the names of the shapes.
3. Demonstrate crayon tracing.
4. Show children how to change the shape into a picture.

Sing and Draw Shapes with the CD, Track 17

Use an easel, flip chart, or board for this activity.

Directions

1. Teach shapes as they appear in the workbook.
2. Let children watch you change shapes into pictures.
3. Let children imitate you. Do not use the CD for this activity.
4. Make very simple drawings step-by-step for them to imitate.

   Note: This activity is designed to give children confidence so that they'll draw more freely.

HELP ME WRITE MY NAME

Children love their names! Do your students recognize their names? Do you see them trying to write their names? How exciting! Teaching a child to write his or her name depends on two things:

1. Age
2. Readiness

To teach developmentally, we suggest teaching name in capitals in preschool and transitioning to name in title case at the end of preschool or the start of kindergarten when children are ready.

Start of Preschool and Start of Kindergarten — NAME

When you think it's time to help a child write letters, start with capitals. Capitals are the easiest to write and recognize. They are all the same height and all start at the same place (the TOP).

Students won't always write in capitals, but it's the easiest way for them to start. You can explain that there are two ways to write a name. The big letter way and the small letter way. Show them both, and then tell them the secret: Their hands are growing and they are ready to learn the big letter way. When they get big and their hands get stronger, they can learn the other way too. Children will follow your lead.

We suggest:

1. Displaying names both ways in the room: all caps and title case (small letter way)
2. Teaching name in all caps through careful demonstration and imitation activities

To Teach NAME in Preschool

1. Use the Capital and Number Practice Strips.
2. Put your strip above the child's strip. Demonstrate each letter on your strip and wait for the child to imitate you. Do this letter by letter (see below).

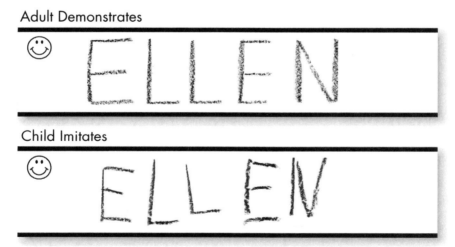

Adult Demonstrates

Child Imitates

End of Preschool and Start of Kindergarten: Name

If you have some students who are doing well with their writing and are interested in learning to write their name in title case, teach them. It is important for them to learn the correct formation habits for the letters in the names, but it is also challenging because they aren't getting the benefit of complete lowercase instruction. So, take some extra time to help them understand the size and formation habits for writing the lowercase letters. Using Wet–Dry–Try on the Blackboard with Double Lines is the best way to teach this. See page 55 of this guide.

Educate Parents

The next page has information we like to send home to parents with some Capital Strips. Visit **www.hwtears.com/click** to get a printable version.

Help Me Write My Name

"That's my name. My name starts with _____." Maybe your child is trying to write or even make letters you can recognize. If so, then it's time to start demonstrating how to write a few letters. Here's how:

1. Be a good example.
2. Write in all capitals.
3. Start every letter at the top.
4. Teach letters step-by-step.
5. Write on paper strips with a smiley face in the top left corner.

How can I be a good example?
Hold the crayon correctly. Your child will be watching how you form letters and hold the crayon or pencil. Be a good model. You may need to make a special effort to hold the crayon correctly.

Why should I use all capitals?
Capitals are the first letters that children can visually recognize and remember. They are the first letters children can physically write. If a child can write his or her name correctly in capitals, you may introduce lowercase letters.

Does it matter where my student starts?
Yes, it does. English has one basic rule for both reading and writing: read and write from top to bottom, left to right. When you write with a child, always start at the top.

What do I say when I teach the letters?
Always say, "I start at the top." Then describe the part you're making. Say "big" or "little" for size. Say "line" or "curve" for shape, like this: **D** = "I start at the top. I make a big line. Now I make a big curve."

What do I use and how do I do this?
Use two strips of paper, one for you and one for the child. Place your strip directly above the child's and demonstrate the first letter in the child's name. Say each step as you make the letter. Be sure the child can see the strokes as you write. (Avoid blocking the child's view with your hand.) Then tell the child to make the letter on his/her paper. Say the steps as the child writes, encouraging the child to say the steps aloud with you. Continue letter by letter.

NOTE:
To Make Paper strips – Use a standard sheet. Fold it in half the long way, and then in half again. Cut on folds to make 4 strips.

Extra help – If the child has difficulty imitating your letter, you may use a gray crayon to pre-write each letter on the child's paper. Do this letter by letter and let the child crayon-trace over your letter. Make your gray letters progressively lighter and discontinue pre-writing as child gains ability.

READINESS INSTRUCTION
YOUR READINESS APPROACH

The right approach to readiness is one that is best for your students, their families, and you. Your goal is to make this year and the next good for your students. You are not just teaching for this year; you are also building a foundation for helping your students transition smoothly to kindergarten.

New Teacher?
If you are a new teacher, study this guide carefully. It will give you important information, guide your approach to teaching, and help you communicate confidently with parents.

Veteran Teacher?
If you are already a strong, experienced teacher, review this guide. You'll find that much of it supports what you already know and do. There are some new things to add to your curriculum and share with parents.

Sharing Your Approach with Parents
Parents look to you for guidance in helping their children develop. You want to share your approach with parents so they will have confidence in you and support your program. At first, they'll judge based on whether their children go to school happily. But then, they'll be asking how their child is progressing and whether the child is in a good program. Share your curriculum so that they will support you and their children. Explain how your preschool environment and program help children develop motor, self-help, and important social-emotional skills.

Sharing Readiness Instruction
Parents are particularly interested in kindergarten readiness. Use the Check Readiness pages in the workbook as an informal readiness check. Give parents the informational pages from this guide and share information about your readiness instruction and goals. You will be helping their children develop these skills through directed play and playful learning experiences. Your readiness instruction will focus on:

Language Skills – Children will be learning names of people, objects, colors, and pictures. They'll know words for size, shape, and positions. They'll use language socially to express needs and interests. They'll use words to tell, ask, explain, compare, and describe.

Coloring/Drawing Skills – Children will be learning to hold the crayon correctly and use the helping hand to hold the paper. They'll progress in coloring skill and be able to name, color, trace, and draw simple shapes. They'll start to draw people and make deliberate marks and strokes.

Letter Skills – You'll teach them the words for capital letter parts (big line, little line, big curve, little curve). They'll learn to recognize capital and lowercase letters. They'll understand about English and books, and that we read and write from top to bottom, left to right. They'll learn to build capital letters correctly in the right sequence. They'll write NAME and be able to trace and write capital letters in their workbooks.

Number Skills – They will know, name and count body parts. They'll learn to observe and count objects and pictures. They will recognize number one to ten and be able to write a few numbers.

Explain that during the year you'll be using a variety of materials and strategies to develop children's readiness skills. Through play and participation, and with activities from the Get Set for School™ curriculum, you will help prepare their children for kindergarten.

Multisensory Lessons

Goodbye to boring lessons. Hello to fun and achievement! Research supports the importance of multisensory teaching to address children's diverse learning styles: visual, tactile, auditory, and kinesthetic. We encourage you to include the multisensory activities in the classroom to appeal to different learning styles and make lessons fun.

The Get Set for School™ program goes beyond typical multisensory instruction. Our strategies and materials are exceptional and uniquely effective at facilitating dynamic classrooms. Here are just a few teaching methods:

Visual
- Step-by-step illustrations of letter formation give clear visual direction.
- Clean, uncluttered black and white pages are presented in a visually simple format.
- Illustrations in workbooks face left to right, promoting left-to-right directionality.

Tactile
- Wet–Dry–Try on a Slate or blackboard gives children touch and repetition without boredom.
- Step-by-step workbook models are big enough for finger tracing.
- The frame of the Slate helps children make lines and keep letters and numbers well proportioned.

Auditory
- Consistent, child-friendly language helps children learn and remember easily.
- Music promotes memorable and entertaining letter instruction.
- Unique letter games prevent children from using old bad habits by delaying the auditory letter cue.

Kinesthetic
- Music and movement teach letter formation.
- Door Tracing and Imaginary Writing teach using large arm movements and visual cues.

We assigned an interactive activity to each letter lesson. Don't be limited by our suggestions. You can use most of the activities with all letters.

Below is the list of our multisensory lessons that are described on the following pages.
- Music and Movement
- Wood Pieces
- Mat Man™
- Roll-A-Dough Letters™
- Stamp and See Screen™
- Door Tracing
- Imaginary Writing
- Wet–Dry–Try
- Magic C*

*These lessons are specific to a group of letters and are included with the letter lessons for each group.

Tips
- Prepare ahead
- Be dynamic and silly
- Sing
- Encourage your students to participate
- Share techniques with parents
- Create your own activities

MUSIC AND MOVEMENT

Music is a big part of our readiness curriculum. You can use the award winning *Get Set For School Sing Along* CD to teach positional concepts, body parts, and letter formation. Whether you are teaching how to build Mat Man or how to count animal legs, this CD has all you need to charge up your lessons and catch your students' attention. The lyrics are on the jacket cover of the CD. The following is a list of suggested activities for each song.

Track #	Song	Suggested Activities
1	**Where Do You Start Your Letters?**	Play a question and answer game with students. Move to the song: reach to the top, bottom, and point to the middle. Share the song with parents.
2	**Alphabet Song**	It is fun to sing ABCs with others in a large group. Follow the children on the CD. They sing every letter clearly, even **L M N O P**! Sing while pointing to Pre-K Wall Cards in the classroom. Sing while pointing to alphabet pages in the *Get Set for School* workbook. Try singing the ABCs with the instrumental version.
3	**Alphabet Song Instrumental**	Sing it on your own!
4	**There's a Dog in School**	Here's a chance to say the alphabet from a dog's point of view. This song will have your students barking the alphabet and laughing at the same time!
5	**Crayon Song**	Children learn to pick up a crayon. Then they gently drop it and do it again. They love to drop. Teaching proper grip has never been so easy or so much fun. Children enjoy learning that their fingers have important jobs!
6	**Magic C**	Making **C**s and circles is easy when the teacher sings and shows children what to do. Children will remember which way to go. Write **C**s and circles in the air.
7	**Hello Song**	It's time to learn this important social skill. Children learn to look, to smile, and to shake hands with the right hand. Now it's easy to know which is the right hand.
8	**Mat Man**	This song helps children build Mat Man as a group. Mat Man teaches body parts, body functions, and simple counting. After building Mat Man, children learn to draw him too.
9	**Count on Me**	It's easy to help children count body parts. We are symmetrically made and our two body parts are on our two sides. The body parts that we have just one of go down the center of our bodies (nose, mouth, belly button).
10	**Five Fingers Play**	Fingers and toes are in units of five. Children count to 5 with this fun fingerplay.

Track #	Song	Suggested Activities
11	**Toe Song**	Children know and love the classic toe play, "This little piggy…" This new song is fun too.
12	**Bird Legs**	No matter what they look like or what they do, birds have two! "**2 4 6 8**, We're counting legs so don't be late!"
13	**Animal Legs**	Play the CD and then make up your own personalized versions with new names and new animals. There are lots of four-legged animals!
14	**The Ant, the Bug & the Bee**	Learn **6** with insect legs. Don't forget to let children fly around like bees.
15	**Spiders Love to Party**	It's fun to sing and dance around the room and think of spiders having **8** legs.
16	**Ten Little Fingers**	Finger–plays are perfect for developing fine motor and imitating skills. This will be a favorite.
17	**My Teacher Draws**	Children love to have grown-ups draw for them. Watching the teacher draw prepares children for drawing.
18	**Puffy Fluffy**	Move to music. Make clouds and rain in the air.
19	**Tap, Tap, Tap**	Use two big lines to tap. Children can follow the rhythm and imitate the teacher's motions.
20	**Golden Slippers (Instrumental)**	Use two big lines for tapping. This upbeat instrumental was added for extra practice tapping. Children can imitate the teacher's movements and tapping patterns. Change movement when the music changes.
21	**Skip to My Lou**	Use this song as a gross motor activity. Each verse has a different gross motor movement. Use this song to teach the concept of start/stop. The music freezes between verses.
22	**Down on Grandpa's Farm**	Sing before taking a field trip to a farm or while learning about arms and animals. Add new verses naming animals and sounds you hear on a farm.
23	**Peanut Butter and Jelly**	Encourage a variety of movements, listening, and following directions.
24	**Rain Song**	Imitate falling rain motions.
25	**Wood Piece Pokey**	Move Wood Pieces up, down, and all around.

Get Set for School Sing Along CD - Music Index by Skill

It's not uncommon for preschool teachers to focus on a specific set of skills. We have cross referenced our songs to help you tailor them to meet your needs.

Songs for Readiness

Track # Alphabet—Writing Skills

1	*Where Do You Start Your Letters?*	Point to the top
2	*Alphabet Song*	Sing ABCs
3	*Alphabet Song (instrumental)*	Sing ABCs
4	*There's A Dog In The School*	Bark and think the ABCs
5	*Crayon Song*	Prepare for holding crayons
6	*Magic C**	Prepare for writing **C** and drawing circles
25	*Wood Piece Pokey**	Learn words for making letters

Body Awareness and Number Skills

7	*Hello Song*	Learn to shake hands with right hand
8	*Mat Man**	Build and draw a person, Numbers 1 + 2
9	*Count On Me*	Body math, Numbers 1, 2, 3, 4, 5, 6, 7, 8, 9, 10
10	*Five Fingers Play*	Fine motor finger–play, 1, 2, 3, 4, 5, 10
11	*Toe Song*	Body math, 5, 10

Fine Motor Skills and Number Awareness

8	*Mat Man**	1, 2—Count body parts
12	*Bird Legs*	2—Count one, two
13	*Animal Legs*	4—Count 2 in front, 2 in back, 4 legs in all, 1 tail
14	*The Ant, The Bug & The Bee*	6—Finger–play, Make 3 + 3 with fingers, Imitate song motions
15	*Spiders Love to Party*	8—Dance, Make 4 + 4 with fingers
16	*Ten Little Fingers*	10—Fine motor finger–play

Drawing Skills

6	*Magic C**	Prepare for writing **C** and circles
8	*Mat Man**	Imitate teacher to draw a person
17	*My Teacher Draws*	Imitate teacher: draw a circle, square and triangle

Listen, Move, and Imitate

18	*Puffy Fluffy*	Move to music: make clouds and rain in the air
19	*Tap, Tap, Tap*	Use two big lines to tap, follow rhythm and the teacher's motions
20	*Golden Slippers*	Use two big lines to follow rhythm and the teacher's motions
21	*Skip to My Lou*	Imitate teacher, stop and start
22	*Down on Grandpa's Farm*	Imitate animal sounds
23	*Peanut Butter and Jelly*	Imitate movements
24	*Rain Song*	Imitate movements
25	*Wood Piece Pokey**	Learn position words with Wood Pieces Set

* These songs appear in more than one category. They help students develop several skills.

More Music - *Rock, Rap, Tap & Learn* CD

Pick up the pace with our *Rock, Rap, Tap & Learn* CD. Use these songs to add variety to some of the multisensory learning activities that are part of the preschool curriculum. Listen to the lyrics for directions on motion and movement. You can find the lyrics to each song in the booklet enclosed with the CD. The songs appropriate for preschoolers are **bold**.

More Songs for Readiness

Track #	Song	Suggested Activities
1	**Alphabet Boogie**	Do a simple boogie to the ABCs.
2	**Where Do You Start Your Letters?**	Play a question/answer game with students.
3	**Air Writing**	Choose a letter and trace it in the air.
4	**Hey, Hey! Big Line**	Use Wood Pieces to review concepts.
5	**Diagonals**	Practice diagonal strokes in the air.
6	**Big Line March**	Use this as a fun introduction to Big Lines.
7	Sentence Song	-
8	My Bonnie Lies Over the Ocean	-
9	Picking Up My Pencil	-
10	Stomp Your Feet	-
11	Vowels	-
12	Frog Jump Letters	-
13	**Give It a Middle**	This song helps children learn **A G H**.
14	**Give It a Top**	Children learn about **I** and **J** and **T**.
15	**Sliding Down to the End of the Alphabet**	Start with **V**, slide all the way to **Z**.
16	**CAPITALS & lowercase**	Emphasize capital and lowercase sizes.
17	Magic C Rap	-
18	Diver Letters School	-
19	Descending Letters	-
20	**Number Song**	Air trace **1-10** in the air.
21	**My Teacher Writes**	Model shapes, letters, and numbers.
22	10 Fingers	-
23	**Mat Man Rock**	Celebrate Mat Man after he is built.
24	**Head & Shoulders, Baby!**	This is a fun way to teach body awareness.
25	**Tapping to the ABC's**	The name says it all!

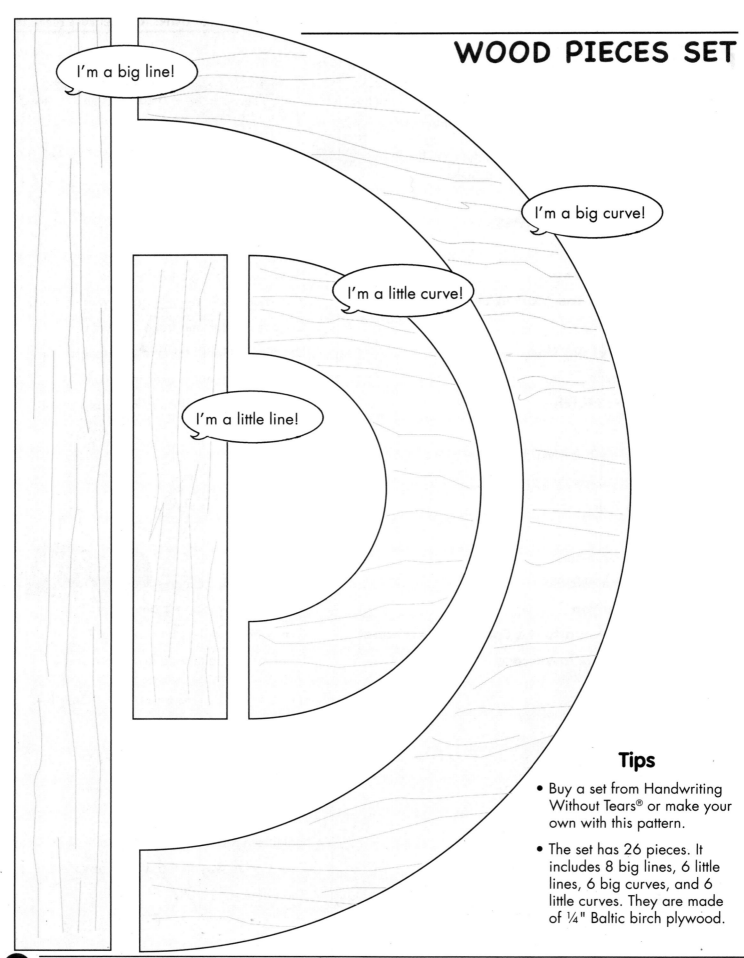

Tips

- Buy a set from Handwriting Without Tears® or make your own with this pattern.

- The set has 26 pieces. It includes 8 big lines, 6 little lines, 6 big curves, and 6 little curves. They are made of ¼" Baltic birch plywood.

Preparing for Wood Pieces

There are several ways the Wood Pieces can be used. Many people besides teachers use the Wood Pieces: parents, tutors, homeschoolers, and therapists. That's because they are highly versatile and can be used in many ways and in many places.

We have some advice for you so that when you use the Wood Pieces, you and your students will get the most out of the experience.

One-on-One
Number of Wood Pieces sets: 1

If seated:
Child sits beside the adult

Small Group
Number of Wood Pieces sets: 1 per 4 children

If seated:
• Children sit in front of the teacher or in a small group on the floor
• Teacher faces the mat for the students' perspective

As a Class
Number of Wood Pieces sets: 1 per 4 children

If seated:
• At their tables or desks with teacher in the front of room
• In a semi-circle on the floor with teacher in the middle

NOTE: If listening to *Get Set For School Sing Along* CD: Students move their bodies around the room and move the wood pieces along to the song.

Introducing Wood Pieces

Working with Wood Pieces is a fun and relaxing way to teach children the concepts and words to describe size and shape. This activity prepares children for making capital letters.

Preparation
Set Wood Pieces in front of children.
Use *Tap, Tap, Tap,* Track 19; *Golden Slippers,* Track 20; and *Wood Piece Pokey,* Track 25 from the *Get Set for School Sing Along* CD.

*Additional Activities:
Rock, Rap, Tap & Learn CD, Hey, Hey!
Big Line, Track 4 and *Big Line March,* Track 6.

Directions
1. Introduce children to the names of the Wood Pieces.
   We are very particular about their names.
   > "This is a big line." (Holding it up in the air.)
   > "Can you show me a big line?" (Children hold it up in the air.)
2. Repeat for other shapes.
   > "This is a little line. Can you show me a little line?"
   > "This is a big curve. Can you show me a big curve?"
   > "This is a little curve. Can you show me a little curve?"
3. Play songs from the CD and have children participate while the music plays.

Skills Developed
1. Language skills
2. Size and shape concepts

Tips
1. You can introduce Wood Pieces to an entire class or to small groups during centers.
2. Don't stop with the activities we suggest. You can create some of your own.

Why Wood Pieces?

How do you teach capital letter **R**? Which verbal directions do you use? If you asked 10 teachers that same question, you would be amazed at the response. Ten different teachers, 10 different responses. Thus, the reason for Wood Pieces. With Wood Pieces, we all say the same thing. You can't beat that type of consistency!

Children learn through consistency. The Wood Pieces allow children to build their capital letters (with exception of **J** and **U**) using 4 basic shapes. By using the Wood Pieces, we can build strong foundation skills for letter memory, orientation, and sequencing.

Beyond learning letters, we also use Wood Pieces to teach children the following:
- Socialization
- Body Awareness
- Prepositions
- Taking Turns
- Motor Movements
- Following Directions
- Stroke Exploration
- Patterns
- Counting

Big Line   Little Curve

Little Line

Polish, Stack, Sort, and Trade Wood Pieces

Children love to feel like they are part of a group. Spread the Wood Pieces on the floor and have children sit around them.

Preparation
1. Scatter Wood Pieces on the floor
2. Gather cloth pieces for polishing

Directions
1. Show children how to polish, stack, and sort the Wood Pieces. This is a friendly, relaxed, and worthwhile activity that they love.
2. Talk about the pieces. Gradually, they will pick up the important words (big line, little line, big curve, little curve) along with the pieces. You can say:

> "You have a big curve. I have a big curve. We picked the same pieces."
> "You have a big line. I have a big curve. Do you want to trade?"
> "Let's polish lines. Do you want to polish a big line or a little line?"
> "It's time to collect the Wood Pieces. Who has a big line?"

Skills Developed
- Size and Shape—Children can feel and see the difference between big and little, line and curve.
- Vocabulary—Children use consistent words (big line, little line, big curve, little curve) to name the pieces.
- Social Skills—Children learn to work together, share, trade, pay attention, and imitate.
- Bilateral Hand Skills—Children develop fine motor skills using one hand to hold as the other rubs. Usually children rub with the dominant hand.
- Visual Skills—Children begin to see the differences in sizes and shapes.
- Figure/Ground Discrimination—Students can find a particular piece in an assortment of scattered pieces.

Tips
1. Use socks on hands to rub the Wood Pieces.
2. Make up songs while rubbing. This one goes to *Row, Row, Row Your Boat*:

Rub, rub, rub big line   Rub, rub, rub big curve
Rub your big line   It is nice and round
Rub, rub, rub big line   Rub, rub, rub big curve
It looks just like mine   Now put it on the ground

Wood Pieces in the Bag
Children learn with a sense of touch.

Preparation
Fill a bag with assorted Capital Letter Wood Pieces.

Directions
1. Child reaches inside, feels one piece, guesses which piece it is, and then takes it out.
2. Teacher names a piece for the child to find.

Skills Developed
- Tactile Discrimination of Size and Shape—Children feel the characteristics of the piece they are touching.
- Vocabulary—Children use consistent words to describe size and shape (big line, little line, big curve, and little curve).
- Fine Motor Skills—Reaching in the bag and manipulating the piece with one hand develops manipulative skills.
- Taking Turns—Waiting for a turn.
- Socialization—Speaking to their neighbors, holding the bag for them.

Tip
- You can easily alter the level of this activity just by changing what you put in the bag. For very young children or those with special needs, put in just two different shapes.
- Make it extra fun by adding objects too, like a ping-pong ball or a spoon. Children will use words that describe the size and shape of these objects.
- Sit in a circle as a class and take turns passing around the bag. Children close their eyes and have to find what their classmate suggests.

Positions in Space and Body Parts with Wood Pieces

Children learn positions and placement skills with Wood Pieces.

Preparation

Each child needs a big line or a little line.

Directions

Say the name of each position or body part as you demonstrate. Have children say it too.

UP in the air
Move it UP and DOWN

UNDER your chair
UNDER your arm (one arm out)
OVER your arm

Out to the SIDE
Move it AROUND in circles

Hold it in FRONT of you
Hold it at the BOTTOM
It's VERTICAL

Climb UP and DOWN
Hold it at the BOTTOM, MIDDLE, TOP

Say HORIZONTAL
Move it SIDE to SIDE

Skills Developed

- Imitating—Children learn to watch and follow the teacher.
- Positioning—Children learn to hold and move the pieces in various positions. They learn the words that describe position.

Tips

- Teach other position words such as: BEHIND my back, BETWEEN my fingers, BESIDE me, THROUGH my arm (put hand on hip first), ON my lap.
- When teaching TOP, BOTTOM, MIDDLE, use a big line. Teacher holds the big line with just one hand at the BOTTOM, then changes hands and positions, naming the position each time. Children imitate.
- Teach body parts by naming each body part as you touch it with a Wood Piece.

More Positions - Vertical, Horizontal, and Diagonal

By imitating you, children learn position and placement skills and words.

Preparation

Give each child the pieces to be used.

Directions

Say the name of each position as you demonstrate. Have children say it too.

Hold two big lines in one hand.

Open them! Hold them out. Say, "Voila! It's a **V**." (Guide child in finger tracing the **V**.)

Hold two big lines end to end diagonally. Move and say, "Diagonal, diagonal."

Make a big line stand up. Make it "walk" on your arm.

Now it's tired. Make it lie down.

One big line is standing up. One little line across the top. It's a **T**.

Hold one big line in each hand.

Put them together at the top. Looks like a teepee or the start of **A**.

Together at the middle—It's **X**! **X** marks the spot!

Skills Developed

- Vertical and Horizontal—Moving the pieces in vertical and horizontal positions prepares children to make capitals **E F H I L T**.
- Diagonal—Moving the lines diagonally prepares children to make capitals **A K M N R V W X Y Z**. They make **V** and **X** and the beginning of **A**.

Tip

- Encourage children to speak with you. The words vertical, horizontal, and diagonal are fun to say with the motions.

Curves and Circles
By imitating you, children learn to associate shapes with movement.

Preparation
Give each child big or little curves.

Directions
Say the name of each position as you demonstrate. Have children say it too.

APART
Hold the big curves apart.

TOGETHER
Bring them together.

Say "O" or "Zeeeero."
Hold them up to your face.
Make circles in the air now.

RAINBOW—hold a big curve up.
Sing *Somewhere Over the Rainbow.*
Hold the big curve with one hand and
then with the other hand make big
curve motions in the air.

SMILE
Hold big curve up to face.
Make smiles in the air.

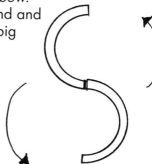

SQUIGGLE—WIGGLE
Hold curves with just one end touching.
Move them alternately up or down.

Skills Developed
- Capitals with Curves—Moving and placing the curves prepares children to write the capitals with curves: **B C D G J O P Q R S**.
- Circle—Children learn that this symbol **O** can be a shape (circle), a letter (**O**) and a number (**O**).
- Associate Movement with Shape—Moving the arm in an arc or circle prepares children for writing curves and circles.

Capitals with Letter Cards

Teach children how to place Wood Pieces on the Letter Cards. Do one to three capitals each session. Use this lesson plan for **F** as a general guide.

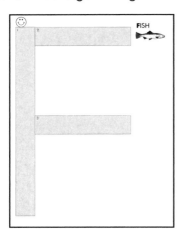 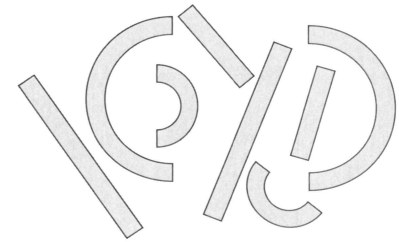

Preparation

Gather Wood Pieces and Letter Cards.

Directions

1. Place the **F** card in front of child.
2. Point to the Letter Card. Say, "This is **F**. **F** starts at the ☺. This word is **FISH**. **FISH** begins with **F**."
3. Describe each step as you place the Wood Pieces on the **F**. "I'm getting a big line to start **F**. I'm putting the big line right here, under the ☺. Now, I'm getting a little line to put at the top. There it is. Now, I'm getting another little line to put at the middle. I made **F**."
4. Remove the pieces.

Try this too...

- When working with a group of children, each child will be making a different letter. Supervise to be sure the pieces are placed in the correct order. Help students notice the number **1** on the card and then select and place that piece first. Follow the numbers to complete each letter correctly.
- When working individually, you may teach planning skills by having a child gather the needed pieces first. Ask, "What do you need to make **F**? First, you need...a big line. How many? One! Get one big line. Then you need...a little line. How many? Two! Get two little lines. You're ready."

Skills Developed

- Letter name for **F**, associating **FISH** with **F**, and the **F** sound
- Finding the Wood Pieces for **F** (1 big line, 2 little lines)
- Placing the Wood Pieces correctly (vertical and horizontal)
- Making the letter **F** in the correct sequence of steps

Tips

- Spreading the pieces randomly creates a figure-ground activity. Choosing the correct piece (figure) from the assortment (ground) helps children develop visual discrimination skills.
- Placing each piece requires fine motor control and spatial (position) awareness. You may help by placing the piece beside the card the way it will be used. Or you may place the piece, take it away, and then let the child try.
- Using cards encourages alphabet awareness. Give each child a card. Have children hold up the cards as the letters are called. Or have children line up alphabetically as the letters are called.

Prewriting and Language Skills with Letter Cards

This side of the card has four beginning activities to teach letter awareness and same/different discrimination. Use this lesson plan for **F** as a general guide.

Preparation
Use the back side of the Letter Cards

Directions
Demonstrate Finding the One that Matches
Row 1. Capital letters made with Wood Pieces
Show children how to point to the first letter. Then demonstrate pointing to each letter in turn, looking for the one that matches. For example:
Show the card. Say, "This page is about the letter **F**."
Point to **F**. Say, "The first letter is **F**. Let's find another **F**."

Point to **D**. Ask, "Is this **F**?...No, no, no. This is **D**. **D** is different."
Point to **E**. Ask, "Is this **F**?...No, no, no. This is **E**. **E** is different."
Point to **F**. Ask, "Is this **F**?...Yes! This is **F**. It is the same letter."

Row 2. Pictures/words that begin with the same capital letter
Show children how to point to the first picture/word. Then demonstrate pointing to each picture/word in turn, looking for the one that matches.
Point to **FISH**. Say, "This is a fish. **FISH** starts with **F**. Let's find another fish."

Point to **FOX**. Ask, "Is this a **FISH**? No, no, no. This is a **FOX**."
Point to **FISH**. Ask, "Is this a **FISH**? Yes! This is a **FISH**. It matches."
Point to **FAN**. Ask, "Is this a **FISH**? No, no, no. This is a **FAN**."

Row 3. Capital letters made with chalk on Slates
Find the capital letter that matches the first one.

Row 4. Printed capital and lowercase letters
Find the capital letter that matches the first one.

Skills Developed
- Letter name for **F** and **f**
- Associating **F** with the **FOX**, **FISH**, **FAN**, and the **F** sound
- Same/different concept
- Important habits: Using a page right side up, from top to bottom and left to right
- Difference between capital **F** and lowercase **f**

Tips
- For children who don't know letters, just do the activity as if you're reading to the child. Encourage participation by following the child's lead.
- Avoid saying "a" or "an" before a letter name. It's confusing to hear "This is a **B**." Simply say, "This is **B**."
- Say "Yes!" enthusiastically and nod your head. Or say "No, no, no" in a cheerful way (like refusing dessert), and shake your head. Children will imitate this.
- The pictures promote left-to-right directionality. See how they face. Move your finger across each row from left to right and encourage children to imitate you.

Capitals with the Mat

Teach children how to make capital letters on the Mat. Unlike the cards, the Mat does not have a letter printed on it. It is simply a bright blue fabric mat (like a mouse pad) with a yellow ☺ in the top left corner.

Preparation
1. Scatter Wood Pieces on the floor in front of children.
2. Give each child a blue Mat.

Demonstrate

Show students how to form the letter piece by piece. Teach in a top-to-bottom, left-to-right order. To see the order for any letter, look in the *Get Set for School* workbook.

Teacher Demonstrates and Student Imitates Piece by Piece

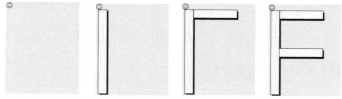

Teach
- When demonstrating, make sure that you make the letter so that it looks right side up from the children's perspective.

What Are We Learning?
- Letter name for **F**
- Finding the Wood Pieces for **F** (one big line and two little lines)
- Making the letter **F** right side up
- Placing the Wood Pieces correctly so **F** is not reversed
- Making the letter **F** in the correct sequence of steps

Tip
- After success with the Mat, teach students with the Roll-A-Dough Letters, the Stamp and See Screen, or the Slate.

Other Wood Piece Activities

Make Letters Together
Children can have fun holding up Wood Pieces and making letters together. Have them try it. They will enjoy figuring out which letters (like the ones that are symmetrical) are easiest to make.

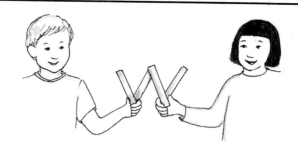

Boss of the Mat
Play the *Boss of the Mat*. Students take turns building capital letters on their Mat and guessing one another's letters. The child who is boss gets to tell each child which Wood Piece to pick up next. The boss places the Wood Pieces one piece at a time (the other children follow) until the letter is called out.

Name
The Wood Pieces are a great way to help children learn the letters in their name. Beginners do well writing their name all in capitals. When they are ready, we transition them to title case. For more information on helping children learn to write their name, see page 27 and 55 of this guide.

What Letter Is It?
This is a great activity to help children with visual memory. Give the child a Mat with Wood Pieces. Have flash cards prepared with lowercase letters on them. Show students a lowercase letter (on the flashcard) and have them build the capital matching partner on their mats.

My Turn, Your Turn
Do a tapping activity with two big lines held like **X**. Teacher taps and students wait to tap until teacher says, "Your turn!" Use just two taps until children learn to listen and wait. When they know how to do this, vary the number or rhythm of taps.

Teacher Says
Play a version of the game "Simon Says" with the Wood Pieces. Remind your children not to do anything unless you say "Teacher Says."
Teacher says, "Touch your big line to your nose."

Making Patterns
You can make many patterns using the Wood Pieces. Download these cards with images of Wood Piece patterns. Glue them to heavy cardstock and laminate. Set them out in a center and see if children can build patterns to match the cards. This is a great visual activity that helps children learn to follow directions and solve problems.

On the Line
Help children understand basic concepts of letter placement by building words with the Wood Pieces and placing them on a line made out of masking tape. Show children how letters sit right on the line.

MAT MAN™

Young children often are asked to draw pictures of themselves or a person. Mat Man makes drawing easy. The following Mat Man activities develop a child's body awareness, drawing, and counting skills.

Preparation

Mat
Wood Pieces:
> 2 big curves (head)
> 3 little curves (ears, mouth)
> 4 big lines (arms, legs)
> 2 little lines (feet)

Accessories:
> 2 hands
> 2 eyes (small water bottle caps)
> 1 nose (large milk or juice cap)
> other items as desired

Directions for Building and Singing

1. Children sit on the floor in a circle.
2. Teacher builds Mat Man on the floor.
3. Teacher gives Mat Man's parts to the children.
4. Children build Mat Man as they sing the Mat Man song with the teacher. (Track 8)
5. Extra accessories (belly button, hair, clothing, seasonal items) will make Mat Man more interesting or change him into a different Mat person.

Directions for Drawing

1. Children sit at tables/desks facing teacher. Teacher draws a large Mat Man at the board or easel.
2. Teacher draws each part in order. Sing/ say: "Mat Man has one head. Watch me draw the head. Now it's your turn!" (Get Set for School Sing Along CD, Track 8)
3. Encourage children to add other details to their drawings.

Skills Developed

- Body Awareness—Body parts, body functions
- Drawing Skills—Placing body parts correctly, sequencing, and organization
- Socialization—Participation, following directions, contributing, taking turns
- Number Awareness—Counting body parts

Tips

- Encourage students to personalize all of their drawings.

A Click Away
hwtears.com/click

Mat Man™

Show children how to build Mat Man using the Mat, Wood Pieces, and a few accessories.

*Additional Activities:
Mat Man Rock, Track 23 of the *Rock, Rap, Tap & Learn* CD.

Mat Man

Tune: *The Bear Went Over the Mountain*

Mat Man has	1 head,	1 head,	1 head,	Mat Man has	1 head,	So that he can*	think
Mat Man has	2 eyes,	2 eyes,	2 eyes,	*(repeat)*	2 eyes,	*(repeat)*	see
Mat Man has	1 nose,	1 nose,	1 nose,		1 nose,		smell
Mat Man has	1 mouth,	1 mouth,	1 mouth,		1 mouth,		eat
Mat Man has	2 ears,	2 ears,	2 ears,		2 ears,		hear
Mat Man has	1 body,	1 body,	1 body,		1 body,	To hold what is inside	heart, lungs, stomach
Mat Man has	2 arms,	2 arms,	2 arms,		2 arms,	So that he can*	reach
Mat Man has	2 hands,	2 hands,	2 hands,		2 hands,	*(repeat)*	clap
Mat Man has	2 legs,	2 legs,	2 legs,		2 legs,		stand
Mat Man has	2 feet,	2 feet,	2 feet,		2 feet,		walk

* Wait for your children to respond. Add extra verses when you add new accessories. Your children may call out other body functions (feet= run, kick, dance). Encourage this while keeping the song/activity moving along.

4-Year-Old: Same Day

4-Year-Old: Same Day

5-Year-Old: Nine Days Apart

Personalize Mat Man™

Below is an example of a child who learned Mat Man in preschool and kindergarten. Eventually she learned that Mat Man can be anyone and started to personalize her drawings of people. You can use this activity with your preschoolers and even help them draw other special people in their lives.

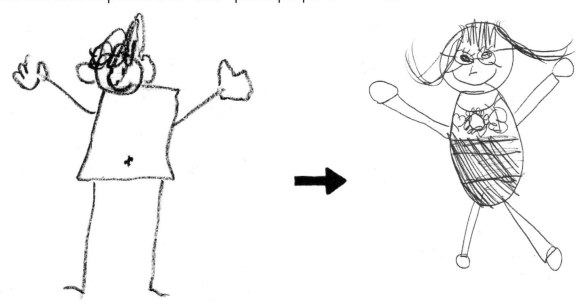

This child's teacher used Mat Man when drawing family portraits. She showed them that girls can have triangles for a dress.

Mat Man™ Pattern

Instructions:
Use these patterns to make body parts with colorful paper. Laminate for durability.

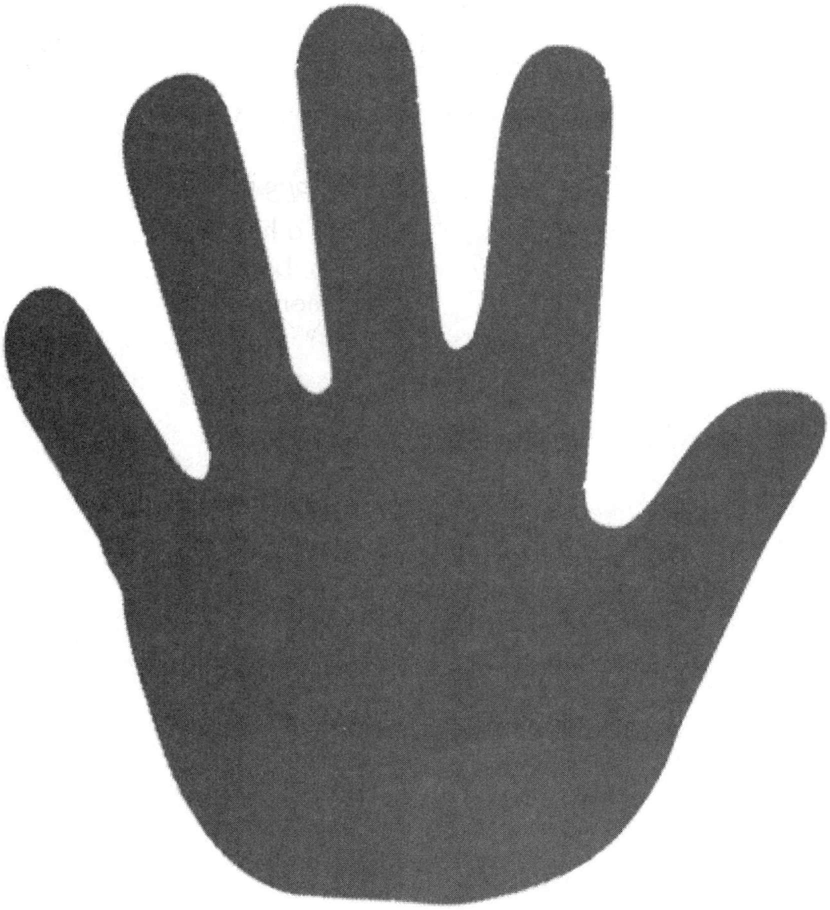

Hand

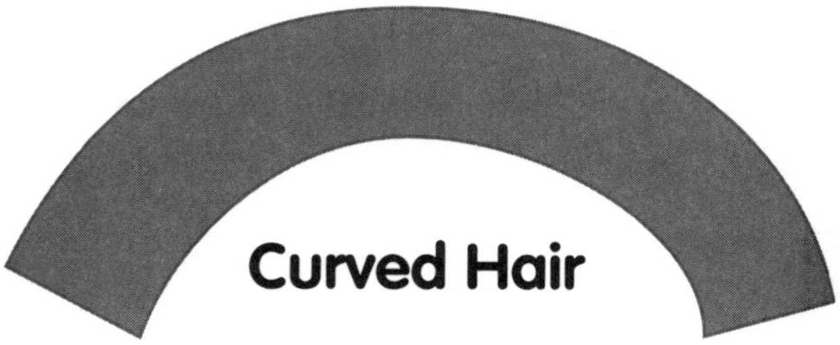

Curved Hair

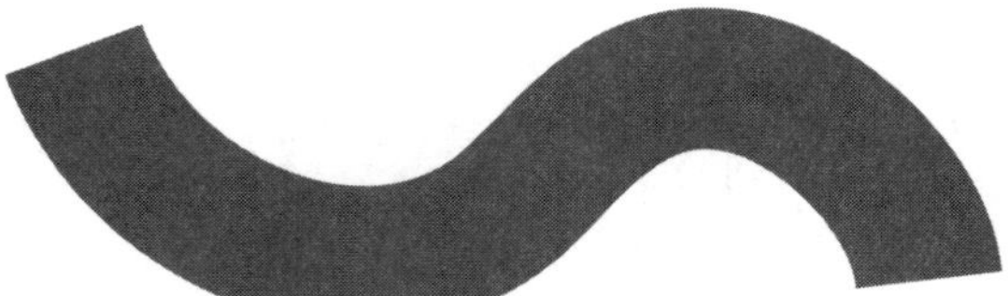

Wavy Hair

Straight Hair

Nose

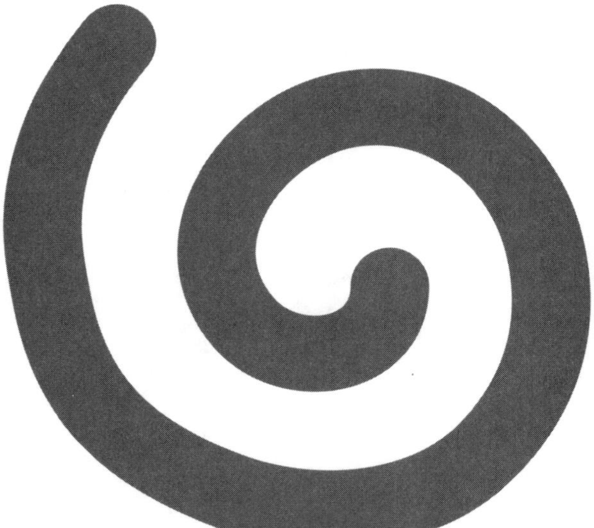

Curly Hair

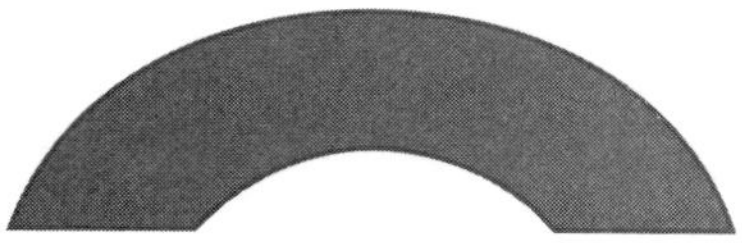

Eyebrow

Eye/Belly Button

MAT MAN SHAPES

There's more that children can do with Mat Man. Your children will enjoy *MAT MAN SHAPES*, a book about what happens when we give Mat Man different shapes. The book has twelve different shapes. You'll enjoy the story and the activities at the back of the book.

Here's a taste of the *MAT MAN SHAPES* book. Ask:
  Can you find MAT MAN with a heart shape?
  Can you find him with an oval body?
  Can you find him with a diamond body?
  Where is the real MAT MAN?
  What is he holding?

Man Man can help your children to compare:

  Circle – Oval

  Square – Rectangle

  Square – Diamond

After you've talked about Man Man and shapes, have the children color the shapes.

Learn more about shapes with our *MAT MAN SHAPES* book *Get Set for School* **67**

ROLL-A-DOUGH LETTERS™

Roll Letters with Me!

Help children form capital letters out of dough. This activity helps children build strength in their fingers and hands while learning capital letter recognition.

Preparation

> Roll–A–Dough Tray
> Dough
> Roll–A–Dough Tray Cards

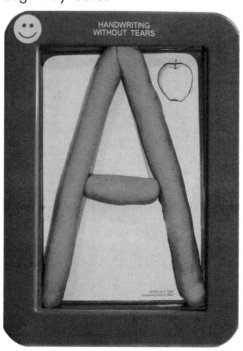

Directions

1. Show how to roll dough (like making a rope or a snake).
2. Children imitate.
3. Teacher shows how to cut and place dough pieces to form a letter. (Use the tray card or just the tray.)
4. Children imitate.

Tips for Teachers

- To see the stroke formation sequence, see page 134 of this guide.
- Use the Roll–A–Dough tray for more sensory experiences with letters. Put shaving cream, sand, pudding, or finger paint in the tray. Then have the child write the capital letter with a finger.

Roll–A–Dough Letters Help Children Develop

- **Fine Motor Skills/Strength**—Rolling and pinching the dough develops the hands
- **Letter Recognition**—Naming the letter
- **Size/Position**—Judging length of the dough piece; Putting pieces on the card or the tray
- **Sensory Exploration**—Multiple sensory experiences help children learn using their senses

STAMP AND SEE SCREEN™
Making Letters on the Stamp and See Screen

Children learn how to make the capital letters step-by-step. The teacher shows how to stamp the pieces in the correct position and sequence. Later children may use the magnetic chalk to write the letter on the screen.

Preparation

Stamp and See Screen
Magnetic big line, little line, big curve, little curve

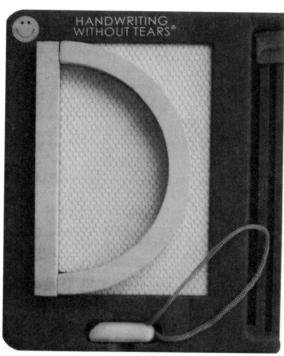

Use the Roll-A-Dough Tray Cards on the Stamp and See Screen to trace.

Directions
1. Teacher stamps the first piece on the screen and then erases it.
2. Children imitate.
3. Teacher stamps the complete letter, step-by-step and then erases it.
4. Children imitate.
5. Children use the magnetic chalk to trace the letter and then they erase it.
6. Children make letter from memory using the pieces or the magnetic chalk.

Tips for Teachers
- Don't erase the screen too quickly. Allow ample time for a student to study the screen.
- Play Mystery Letter game: First person stamps a big line on the left edge of screen. The other person makes a Mystery Letter by stamping pieces on the right side. The first person doesn't know what the letter will be.
- Use the Roll-A-Dough Tray Cards. Choose a card, place it on the magnetic screen, have your student trace over the letter with the magnetic chalk. Remove the card to see the letter on the screen. Student retraces now.
- Play Boss of the Board. The boss gets to decide which letter or number to stamp on the board. This works best with two boards. The first student makes the letter and the second student imitates.

Stamp and See Screen Helps Children Develop
- **Letter Recognition**—Naming the letter
- **Organization**—Choosing the pieces to make the letter
- **Directionality**—Top-to-bottom, left-to-right habits
- **Sequencing**—Making letters step-by-step in correct order
- **Visual Perception**—Visual memory of each step as it's erased
- **Listening Skills/Imitation**—Following teacher directions/demonstrations
- **Sound/Letter Association**—Letter sound for each letter

WET–DRY–TRY

Using the Wet–Dry–Try method, your students will learn to form capital letters correctly without reversals. This activity appeals to all learning styles and is a fun way to practice letters.

Slate Chalkboard

Preparation
1. Prepare Slate Chalkboard with the letter you will be teaching.
2. Place Little Chalk Bits and Little Sponge Cubes around the room so children can reach them easily.

Directions

Teacher's Part
Demonstrate correct letter formation.

Student's Part

WET	**DRY**	**TRY**
• Wet Little Sponge Cube. • Squeeze it out. • Trace the letter with the sponge. • Wet your finger and trace again.	• Crumple a little paper towel. • Dry the letter a few times. • Gently blow for final drying.	• Take a Little Chalk Bit. • Use it to write the letter.

Tips
- Use consistent words to describe the strokes. Match your verbal cues to the directions on the letter lesson pages of the workbook.
- Use Little Sponge Cubes and Little Chalk Bits to help children develop proper pencil grip.
- Squeeze the sponge well or the letter will be too wet.
- This works best one-on-one or in centers with five or fewer students.
- To use this activity with the whole class, pre-mark students' slates with the capital letter (so they have a correct model to wet), and then demonstrate once for everyone.

Other Activities

In addition to doing the Wet–Dry–Try activity with a letter, you can help children with reversals, names, and more. Below are some easy, fun exercises to get started.

Transition Name, Phone Numbers, and Words to paper:
Help children write name, phone number, and words on paper.
1. Prepare Slates with student's name or phone number.
2. Student can Wet–Dry–Try over the numbers.

3. Practice on Gray Block Paper.

GRAY BLOCKS – FOR LETTERS, WORDS OR NUMBERS

Tip for Teaching Name in Title Case

Names
Demonstrate/Imitate: Title Case (Two Blackboards with Double Lines)
1. Prepare two Blackboards with Double Lines.
2. Demonstrate the child's name on one board, as the child imitates on the other.

This activity helps children learn to write their names on double lines before transitioning to paper.

DOOR TRACING

Take advantage of the 🙂 by placing it on the door to help children write capitals and numbers. The 🙂 prevents reversals and promotes the top-to-bottom habit.

Expanding Smiley Face Secrets

Preparation
1. Copy, color, cut, and laminate the smiley face on the following page.
2. Place it in the top left corner of your classroom door.

Directions
1. While teaching, use your door frame to model letter or number formation for your students.
2. Have children air trace capital letters and numbers on the door.

Skills Developed
This activity gives children extra practice with the orientation, formation, and starting position. Air Tracing uses large arm movements for visual and kinesthetic learning.

Tips
Children can trace a letter or number before lunch, at recess, or before leaving at the end of the day.
- Consider having a daily or weekly leader who gets to model for the others.
- Use your door to teach parents about HWT smiley face secrets.
- Have students partner and play Mystery Letter games with Frog Jump and Magic C capitals.
- Play Boss of the Door. The boss gets to decide which letter or number to trace on the door. A good boss traces well enough so that others can guess the letter.

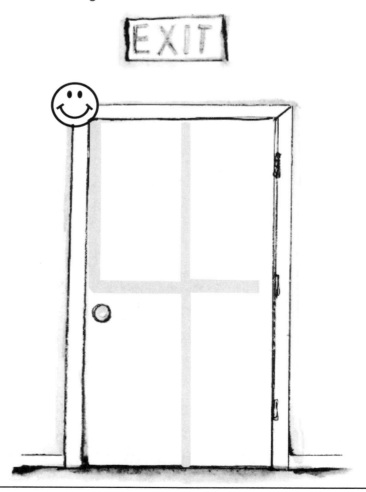

IMAGINARY WRITING

Imaginary Writing is a kinesthetic strategy with visual and auditory components. The picking up and holding of crayons adds a tactile component. This strategy allows you to watch the entire class and ensure that all students are making letters correctly.

Air Writing

Preparation

Learn *Air Writing*, Track 3, from the *Rock, Rap, Tap & Learn* CD.

Directions

1. Sing to prepare the class for participation.
2. Review a letter or number. Trace it in the air in front of your class.
3. Have students hold a crayon correctly in the air. Everyone checks crayon grips.
4. Retrace the letter or number again with your students.

Tip

If you are facing your students, make the letter backward in relation to you so that the letter will be correct from your students' perspective.

My Teacher Writes

Preparation

Gather chalk or markers for a large board or easel. Use *My Teacher Writes*, Track 21, from the *Rock, Rap, Tap & Learn* CD.

Directions

1. Children sing as you stand in front of the class:
   My teacher writes a letter (number) for me
   What's this letter (number) let's look and see
2. Review a letter or number and trace it in the air or on the board.
3. Have students hold a crayon correctly in the air. Everyone checks crayon grips.
4. Retrace the letter or number again with your students.

Tip

If you are facing your students and doing Air Writing, make the letter backward in relation to you so the letter will be correct from your students' perspective.

Follow the Ball

Preparation

Find a brightly colored cup or ball.

Directions

1. Have students hold a crayon correctly in the air. Everyone checks crayon grips.
2. Face the class and hold up a cup or ball.
3. Have students point their crayons at the cup or ball.
4. Write the letter in the air slowly, giving the directions.
5. Have students follow along with their crayons, saying the directions with you.

Tips

- If you are facing your students, make the letter backward in relation to you so that the letter will be correct from your students' perspective.
- Hold the cup or ball in your right hand, out to your right side at eye level. Stand still.
- Say the steps and letters, perhaps: "Big line, big line, little line. This is capital **A**."

Laser Letters

Preparation

Gather a laser pointer and chalk or markers for a large board or easel.

Directions

1. Write a large letter on a board or easel, giving step-by-step directions.
2. Have students hold a crayon correctly in the air. Everyone checks crayon grips.
3. Move to the back of room, and point the laser to the start of the letter.
4. Have students point their crayons to the laser dot at the start of the letter.
5. Use the laser to trace the letter slowly, giving step-by-step directions.
6. Have students follow with their crayons, saying the directions along with you.

Note: You may decide to allow students to use the laser with your supervision.

Tips

Laser letters are ideal for teaching tricky letters because they enable children to see the following:

- You writing the large letter first
- The laser pointing to the start of the completed letter
- The laser moving along the completed letter

Crayon, Chalk, and Pencil Skills
DEVELOPMENTAL STAGES IN WRITING READINESS

Using a writing tool correctly requires instruction. Correct grips need to be taught. Awkward grips just happen. How children hold the crayon, chalk, or pencil depends on their developmental stage, the writing tool being used, and the instruction the students receive. Here is a general guide of how children develop with proper instruction and practice.

2-year-old: scribble mark, vertical line, horizontal line

Writing hand/arm: Child uses all fingers to hold crayon in palm of the hand. Arm is in the air expressing anticipation.

Helping hand/arm: Has no purposeful use.

Present skill: Child makes random contact with the paper.

Next skill: Show child how to make scribbles, lines down and lines across.

3-year-old: circle, cross

Writing hand/arm: Child uses all fingers to hold crayon in the palm of the hand. Arm is down on the table, but not well planted.

Helping hand/arm: Child is just starting to use the helping hand.

Present skill: Copies lines down and lines across

Next skill: Show child how to make a circle and cross.

Developing Motor Skills for Twos and Threes

Outside—Use playground equipment, swings, slides, big push and riding toys, sandbox play, and balls.

Inside—Building blocks teach controlled release. Nesting toys engage both sides of the body. Toy trains, animals, and cars teach manipulating skills. Puzzles teach visual discrimination and placing skills. Pictures encourage pointing. Avoid high tech toys and stick with the classics.

Daily Life—Encourage undressing (easier) and dressing, washing hands, and brushing teeth. Eating small food pieces helps children practice picking up very little things. Have children help with simple take-out and put-away tasks.

4-year-old: square, triangle

Writing hand/arm: Mature grasp begins to emerge (using thumb with 1 or 2 fingers). Notice the elbow. It's up. This is arm writing. The hand moves freely in the air.

Helping hand/arm: Child starts holding the paper deliberately.

Present skill: Child copies line down, line across, circle and cross

Next skill: Show this child how to make a square and a triangle. Show the child how to trace letters and numbers. Help with holding a crayon. Use stencils. Holding the stencil still helps a child develop the helping hand. Continue with free exploration.

5-year-old: diamond

Writing hand/arm: Use mature grasp. This is hand writing. The hand rests on the paper.

Helping hand/arm: Child purposely uses the hand to hold and place the paper.

Present skill: Child copies a cross, circle, square, and triangle.

Next skill: Child begins to draw circle, square, and triangle independently. Show this child how to draw a diamond and how to write letters and numbers. Help with holding a crayon if needed. Encourage drawing.

Developing Motor Skills for Fours and Fives

Outside—Continue previous activities. Add simple games and building projects.

Inside—Continue previous activities. Finger painting, easel work, and drawing with little pieces of chalk or crayon develop coordination and holding habits. Finger–plays, music and imitating build body awareness. Play dough, toys with small pieces, and simple crafts like bead stringing help children develop fine motor skills.

Daily Life—Continue previous activities. Add more helping tasks that use precise fine motor control: pouring, spreading, setting table.

FINE MOTOR SKILLS AND STRENGTH

Developing fine motor skills is one of the most important parts of a preschool teacher's job. Here are new and familiar activities for encouraging fine motor skills.

Finger–Plays
Use familiar finger–plays and new finger–plays from the *Get Set for School Sing Along* CD.
- *The Ant, The Bug and The Bee* (see page 71, Track 14)
- *Spiders Love to Party* (see page 121, Track 15)
- *Five Fingers Play* (see page 111, Track 10)
- *Ten Fingers* (see below)

Ten Little Fingers
I have ten little fingers and they all belong to me
I can make them do things, Just you wait and see
I can wiggle them high, And wiggle them low
I can push them on the floor, And stretch them just so
They can make little Os, If I touch them together
They can even make a cup, To catch rain in rainy weather
I can stretch them out wide, Or close them real tight
I might just fold them quietly, When I sleep at night

Suggested Activity
- Use this song to warm up the hands. This song helps children to move their fingers in a variety of ways.
- Use as finger–play any time of day.

Toys
We live in a world of technology. Toys are different today than they were several years ago. They light up, talk, and play music at the push of a button. Even many educational toys do not give the child anything to do beyond pushing buttons. Be picky about the toys you choose. Select toys that require children to use hand skills to move pieces, manipulate parts, or snap things together.

Easel Activities
Vertical surfaces are great for developing hand skills. Other vertical surfaces include mirrors, windows, walls (tub walls too), and refrigerators. The best part about a vertical surface is that children create their own working space at just the right height! When a child's arms and hands are positioned upward working against gravity, they are building strength in the shoulders and arms. Also, a child's wrist is forced into a neutral position, which is the position that is used later, when the child begins to write. For more ideas on easel activities turn to page 18.

Playing with Dough Letters
Preschoolers love to play with dough. Most enjoy touchy/feely sensory experiences. Use the Roll–A–Dough Letters to encourage fine motor skills and hand strength. For directions on this activity turn to page 52.

Playground Play
Did you know that most children's upper body strength and motor coordination develop through play? The use of playground equipment is a great way to help a child develop the strength and coordination required for fine motor skills. Some children may never have the opportunity to use playground equipment. Allow time in your day for children to experience the benefits of monkey bars, swings, and other great playground equipment.

Educating Parents
Parents are a child's most important teacher. Parents love to help their children learn. Educate parents about preschool activities by sending home the parent articles in the back of this guide. It's amazing what good habits can be taught to children when we all work together.

THE HELPER HAND

The Role of the Helper Hand

The helping hand positions and holds the paper. The helping hand helps maintain good posture while children write. To develop handwriting skill efficiently, children need to use the helping hand consistently.

Developing Dominant and Helping Hands

Some activities, like eating with a spoon, use just one hand. They are unilateral activities. Other activities use two hands and are called bilateral activities. Some bilateral activities, like pushing a cart or holding on to a swing use the hands in the same way. Neither hand develops superior skill. But other bilateral activities, like stringing beads, use the hands for different purposes. The dominant hand develops superior skill while the other hand is used as a holding hand. These activities are good for both hands. It is important to provide bilateral activities that train a child to use a helping hand. These activities prepare for handwriting by requiring them to use the helping hand. Here are a few:

- Holding a container of bubble soap while dipping the wand and blowing bubbles
- Holding a bowl and stirring
- Holding beads and stringing them
- Holding a funnel and spooning sand into the funnel
- Holding a box of something and taking things out
- Holding a flower and picking petals

Encouraging Children to Use the Helper Hand

1. HWT suggests these activities that require using the helping hand:
   - Wood Pieces—Hold a Wood Piece and rub it with the other hand.
   - Slate—Hold a slate steady on the table and write on it with chalk.
   - Stencils, shapes, and rulers—Hold them steady with one hand while marking with the other.
   - Hand tracing—Hold one hand flat while the other hand traces around it.

2. When preparing children for writing, be sure to tell them to hold the paper with a flat helping hand. Keeping the hand flat helps children stay relaxed when they write.

3. If children ignore the helping hand when coloring or starting to write, try this:

   Give the helping hand a name. Ask a child to choose a name, one that starts with the same letter as his or her name. Then talk directly to the hand (not the child) and call the hand by the new name. Tell the helping hand to help the child. Tell the hand to hold the paper. Children think it's funny when you talk to the hand. They don't get embarrassed because it's the helping hand, not them, that's being corrected.

Use Your Oven Rack

You may never have thought that your oven rack could be so handy. You can help a child learn vertical and horizontal lines by using your oven rack. Plop the rack on a large sheet of paper, hand the child a crayon, and let it make lines back and forth. By holding the rack with the other hand, the child is getting practice using the helping hand for stabilization.

HOLD ON...YOU HAVE TO TEACH GRIP

Research shows that close to 50 percent of three-year-olds have the fine motor ability to hold a small crayon correctly.* But the correct grip has to be taught. You can end awkward or even fisted pencil grips by using direct teaching and certain strategies. Young children are pliable—they can be molded gently into good habits. Here are strategies for you to use when teaching a correct crayon grip.

Handedness

If a child is truly undecided by the time handwriting training begins, choose the hand that is more skilled to be the writing hand. Without a dominant hand, experience and training is divided between two hands and children develop nearly equal hand skills. But they are not as skilled with one hand as their peers who have given a dominant hand more training. To determine which hand is most skilled, take the functional approach. A teacher, parent, and occupational therapist (if available) should observe the child. Watch how the child colors, draws, writes, zips a jacket, eats, etc. This will allow all of the observers to determine which hand appears more skilled. Once a dominant hand is determined, encourage the child to use the more skilled hand during writing tasks. Placing utensils, crayons or chalk on that side will help.

*Research found on page 132.

Little Crayons/Little Pencils

With all the fun writing tools available today, it's hard to decide which age is appropriate. The best tool for preschool children is the crayon. Crayons create a natural resistance and build strength in the hand. They prepare the hand for using a good pencil grip.* Our Flip Crayons are the perfect tool. They are designed with dual colors and dual tips to encourage fine motor development: when a children flip the crayons, they are using in-hand manipulation skills. These skills lead to improved coordination. Don't promote pencil use too much. Children will get plenty of practice using pencils in kindergarten when their hands are ready. When moving a child to a pencil, use a golf-size pencil. Children will do better with a short pencil that's in proportion with the size of their hands. Avoid fat primary pencils because they are too heavy and long for little hands. Markers are fine when used in moderation.

Demonstrate Grip

The time to teach proper grip is when a child becomes interested in coloring. Show children how to hold their crayons correctly by demonstrating finger placement and modeling a correct grip.

Standard and Alternate Grip

The standard grip, also called the "tripod grip," uses three fingers for holding the crayon or pencil. The thumb is bent, the index finger is pointing to the tip of the crayon, and the crayon rests on the side of the middle finger. The last two fingers are curled in the palm and give the hand stability.

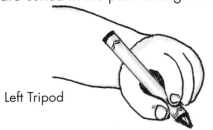

Left Tripod

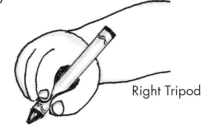

Right Tripod

An alternative grip, called the quadropod grip (four fingers) is another way children may hold their crayon. The thumb is bent, the index and middle finger point to the tip of the crayon and the crayon, rests on the ring finger. This grip is efficient and does not need to be corrected.

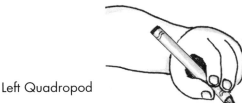

Left Quadropod

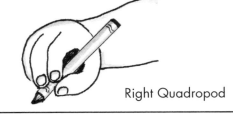

Right Quadropod

Teach the Correct Pencil Grip in Three Easy Steps

This step-by-step technique is a great way to develop a correct pencil grip or to fix an awkward one. The trick is that you teach the grip in three separate stages. At first, you help children pick up the crayon and hold it correctly. That's all. Next, you show them how to aim the crayon and scribble on paper. Then, you teach them how to make deliberate strokes.

1. **Pick Up** (Remember they don't write at this stage. Don't even have paper on the table.)
   Tell the children to pick up their crayons and hold them in the air! Help them place their fingers correctly. Then say, "Wow, that is just right! Let's take the crayons for a ride in the air." Now tell them to gently drop the crayons. Do it again. Sing the *Crayon Song* when you do this activity. Continue with this activity until children can automatically pick up and hold crayons correctly.

2. **Aim and Scribble** (Use blank paper with a dot like this • or start the *Get Set for School* workbook.)
   Tell children to aim the crayon and put it on the dot or star. The little finger side of the crayon hand should rest on the paper. Some children will need help putting down the crayon hand. Don't forget the helping hand. It has to be flat and resting on the paper. Now it's time to scribble. Don't lift the crayon or hand, just wiggle and scribble. The beauty of this step is that children develop their crayon grip and finger control without being critical of how the writing or drawing looks.

3. **Color/Trace/Draw** (Use *Get Set for School* workbook.)
   Have children pick up a crayon and use it for workbook pages or free drawing. Continue using previous steps as needed to reinforce the correct habits. This will get your students off to a wonderful start.

Pencil Grips

At a young age, children are motivated to learn new skills. If they are holding a crayon or small pencil incorrectly, demonstrate the proper grip for them and try the techniques described above or on page 64. Avoid using pencil grips or any other type of adaptive writing device for preschoolers. A physical device cannot substitute for a child being taught how to hold the crayon or pencil. Pencil grips are for older children who find them helpful.

Introduce Fingers

Children need to know their fingers so that they can follow your directions. Start by naming the fingers that hold the crayon. Here is how to introduce them:

Thumb— Everyone, hold up your thumb. Say "Hi" to your thumb. "Hi thumb."

Pointer— Hold up your pointer finger. Wiggle it around. Say "Hi" to pointer finger. "Hi pointer."

Middle— Hold up middle finger next to pointer. Middle finger is taller than the pointer finger. We call him "Tall Man" because he is the tallest finger.

Now say, "Your fingers have very important jobs to do. I'm going to teach you a song so you can remember their jobs."

Crayon Song

Pick up a crayon, Pick up a crayon, This is easy to do
Pick up a crayon, Pick up a crayon, I just tell my fingers what to do
My thumb is bent, Pointer points to the tip, Tall Man uses his side
I tuck my last two fingers in and take them for a ride

Now I'm holding it just right, But not too tight, Every finger knows what to do
And now I have a big surprise, A big surprise for you
Let's drop it and do it again!

NOTE: Use the CD just to learn the tune. Then use the song without the CD while teaching. As you are singing the song, it's very important to walk around the room and position children's fingers for them correctly on the crayon. It will take several repetitions before children will pick up the habit naturally.

Why Children (and Teachers) Succeed with HWT
PRE-STROKE, LETTER, AND NUMBER STYLE

Strokes — Pre-Strokes, Shapes, Letters, and Numbers

In preschool, children start to make deliberate single strokes with control. Some strokes are developmentally easier to write than others.* Children gradually develop their ability to copy forms in a very predictable order. The *Get Set for School* workbook teaches strokes to children based on the following order:

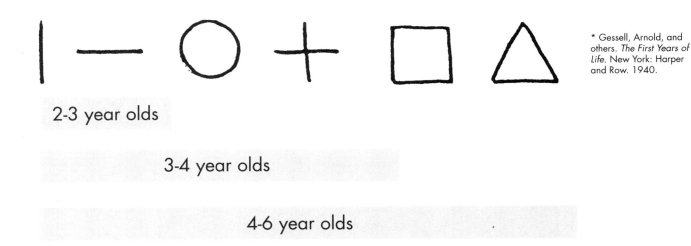

* Gessell, Arnold, and others. *The First Years of Life.* New York: Harper and Row. 1940.

2-3 year olds

3-4 year olds

4-6 year olds

A Workbook with Unique Crayon Strokes

HWT has designed the unique gray crayon stroke. After trying various tracing methods, we found that this is the easiest stroke for children to trace.

...with Easy Starts and Stops

In the Get Set for School™ program, the crayon stroke letters and numbers are That's because each letter has a starting symbol to cue children where to put start the letter. It may be a ☺ or an ⇩. To prepare, the children simply place by the starting icon and then follow the gray crayon stroke. All letters and at the top, so starting and stopping are easy. The page stops! Take a look or number page. See how the letters are placed at the bottom of the page. that they aren't supposed to write on the table. They see the page ending to slow down and stop.

Say No to Dot-to-Dot

Dot-to-dot letters don't work because children focus on the dots, just going from one dot to the next. They learn to follow dots, but they don't learn the strokes. Crayon strokes are seen as complete strokes. Children follow and learn the basic strokes easily. There is a surprise too. When children trace over the strokes, the underlying gray strokes disappear! The page shows just the child's letters or numbers. Children are so proud, so they feel proud of their work.

Simple
Crayon Stroke

Confusing
Dot-to-dot

UNIQUE WORKBOOK FEATURES

A Workbook that Scribbles, Colors, and Teaches Control

Tell children to aim the crayon and put it on the dot or star. The little finger side of the "crayon hand" should rest on the paper. Some children will need help putting down the crayon hand. Don't forget the helping hand. It has to be flat and resting on the paper. Now it's time to scribble. Don't lift the crayon or hand, just wiggle and scribble. This step helps children develop their crayon grip and finger control without criticism of how the writing or drawing look. They can use their newly acquired crayon grip on the coloring pages. Each coloring page teaches color and shape recognition as well as language skills.

Aim and Scribble page

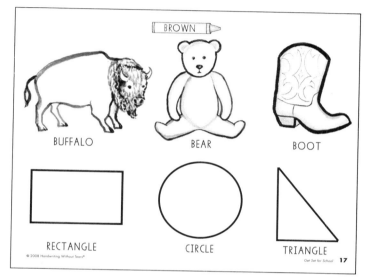

Coloring page

Children learn how to steer the crayon with pre-stroke pages, which are fun and give lots of practice in moving the crayon. Children may trace the crayon lines over and over as they learn to make vertical, horizontal, curved, or diagonal lines. These pages are appealing and easy to do. They prepare children for correctly tracing and learning how to make shapes, letters, and numbers. Crayon skills continue to be refined with coloring and children develop more control for starting and stopping strokes. Note: The HWT readiness activities (easel, Mat Man, build and draw) develop skill, confidence, and interest in drawing. Children are encouraged to add their own finishing touches and extra drawings to all the workbook pages.

A Workbook with Consistent Words

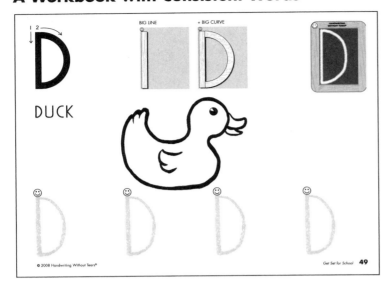

Get Set for School uses consistent, simple words to teach capital letters. It's easy to learn letters when all adults use the same child-friendly words. How do you talk about letter **D**? Look at the illustration of making the **D** with Wood Pieces and say, "**D** starts with a big line and then we add a big curve." This language is simple for children and teachers, whether they're making **D** with Wood Pieces, **D** with chalk on the Slate, or **D** with a crayon in the workbook. What about **P**? **P** has a big line and a little curve. What about **L**? **L** has a big line and then a little line at the bottom. Simple consistent words: big line, little line, big curve, little curve make it easy for children to follow your step-by-step directions. Teach capital letters confidently and consistently with the Wood Piece words.

A Workbook that Teaches Lowercase Recognition

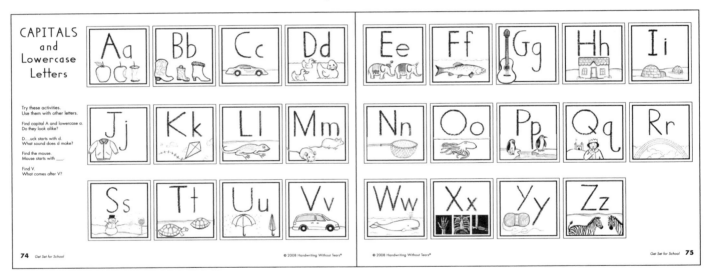

Capital letters prepare children for lowercase letters Children recognize the capital/lowercase partners.
Cc   Oo   Ss   Vv   Ww   Xx   Zz

Children recognize the similar lowercase letters:
Jj   Kk   Pp   Tt   Uu   Yy

Children recognize different letters:
Aa   Bb   Rr   Ii   Ee   Dd   Nn
Ff   Mm   Hh   Gg   Ll   Qq

Children practice with the Lowercase Matching activity: They see **A a - g a**. They know that **a** is **A**. They learn to name, match, and circle lowercase **a**.

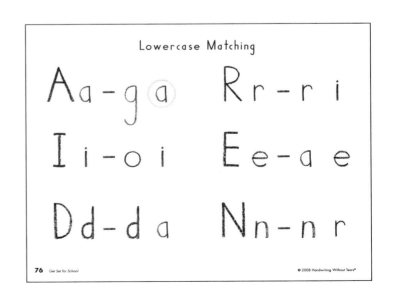

A Workbook that Counts

Each number page has a related counting activity. Children make numbers **1—5** with fingers, Wood Pieces and the Slate. They also color the pictures and trace the crayon stroke numbers. Numbers **6—10** have pictures to count. The workbook pages for numbers **2, 4, 6,** and **8** directly relate to songs on the *Get Set for School Sing Along* CD. All of this adds up to a successful experience for the child who'll be entering kindergarten..

A Workbook that Checks Readiness

At the back of every child's *Get Set for School* workbook is an informal readiness check. Many preschools already have a system for recording progress and sharing information. This one has very specific kindergarten readiness tasks. Use it as you think best. Here are some suggestions:

- For a few, or all students.
- At the beginning of the year, during the year, or near the end of the year.
- To record information and progress
- To plan lessons and activities
- To share with parents

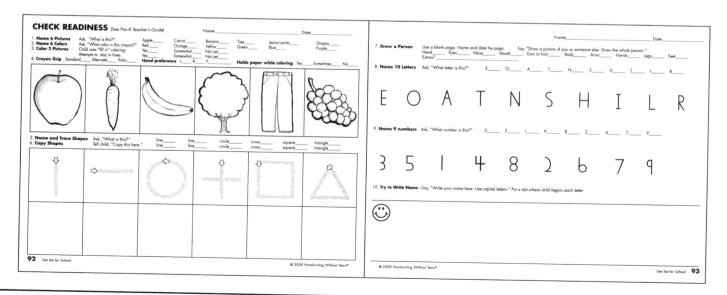

CRAYON SKILLS

Night Sky—Aim and Scribble

Ask
Have you ever seen stars in the sky?
What color are they? What color is the moon?
Have you ever seen a firefly? When do fireflies come out?

Begin to look and learn
Let's find fireflies. (Point) Let's find stars. (Point)
Let's find the moon. (Point)

Color
Let's sing the *Crayon Song* (see page 65).
Let's color the moon yellow.

Demonstrate
Let's scribble stars. Put the crayon on the star. Scribble.
Let's scribble fireflies. Put the crayon on the firefly. Scribble.

Extra
Look at other pictures of fireflies.

Twinkle—Aim and Scribble

Ask
Do you sleep under a quilt? What color is it?
Have you ever seen stars in the sky? What color are they?

Begin to look and learn
Let's find the quilt. (Point) Let's find stars. (Point)

Color
Let's color the quilt.

Demonstrate
Let's scribble stars. Put the crayon on the star. Scribble.

Extra
Sing *Twinkle, Twinkle Little Star*.

Fireworks—Aim and Scribble

Ask
Have you ever seen fireworks? What color are they?
Do we see fireworks during the day or at night?

Begin to look and learn
Let's find fireworks. (Point)
Let's find the children. (Point)

Color
Let's color the children.

Demonstrate
Let's scribble fireworks. Put the crayon on the center of
the firework. Scribble.

Extra
Look at pictures of fireworks.

A Click Away
hwtears.com/click

Activity Page – AIM AND TRACE

Get Started Say, "Do you see the ant, the bug, and the bee? Let's color them and trace the lines."

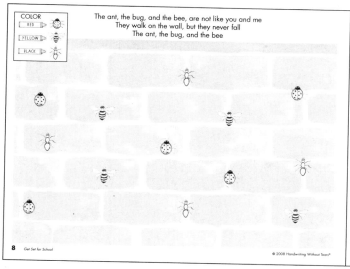

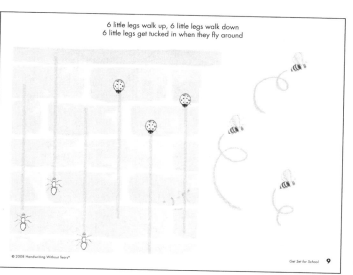

How do I teach this?

Ask
Have you ever seen ants? What color are they?
Have you ever seen ladybugs? What color are they?
Have you ever seen bees? What color are they?

Begin to look and learn
Play and sing *The Ant, The Bug and The Bee*.
Let's find ants. (Point)
Let's find ladybugs. (Point)
Let's find the bees. (Point)

Color
Color the ants, the bugs, and the bees.

Demonstrate
Let's trace lines up, down, and all around. Put the crayon on the ant. Line goes up. Put the crayon on the ladybug. Line goes down. Put the crayon on the bee. Line goes all around.

Extra
Sing the song *The Ant, The Bug, and The Bee*. Have the children put their hands together with three fingers up on each hand. Then crawl fingers up and down and all around. Fly around like bees.

Coloring Pages – RED AND GREEN

Get Started
Help children choose a RED and a GREEN crayon or the RED/GREEN FLIP Crayon™ to color these pages. With just five Flip Crayons, they'll have the ten colors they need. Skipping back and forth between these pages gives children fine motor and grip practice by flipping or switching crayons. Show the similarity between the pictures and shapes below them. For example, the STOP sign is an octagon.

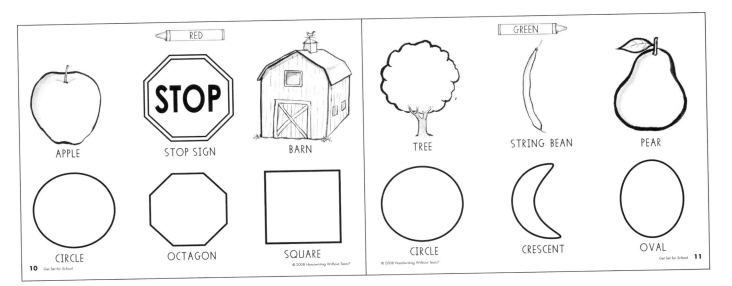

Red
Ask about red
Can you find the crayon? (Point)
Let's color the crayon red.
Do you know anything that is red?

Begin to look and learn
Let's find the apple. (Point)
Let's find the stop sign. (Point)
Let's find the barn. (Point)
Let's find the circle. (Point)
Let's find the octagon. (Point)
Let's find the square. (Point)

Color
Let's sing the *Crayon Song* (see page 65).
Color the apple, stop sign, and barn red.
Color the shapes below red.

Demonstrate
Let's trace shapes. Put finger on shape and trace.

Extra
Point to red items in the room.

Green
Ask about green
Can you find the crayon? (Point)
Let's color the crayon green.
Do you know anything that is green?

Begin to look and learn
Let's find the tree. (Point)
Let's find the string bean. (Point)
Let's find the pear. (Point)
Let's find the circle. (Point)
Let's find the crescent. (Point)
Let's find the oval. (Point)

Color
Color the tree, string bean, and pear green.
Color the shapes below green.

Demonstrate
Let's trace shapes. Put finger on shape and trace.

Extra
Point to green items in the room.
Mix blue and yellow to make green.
Eat green snacks.

Coloring Pages – YELLOW AND PURPLE

Get Started

Help children choose YELLOW and PURPLE crayons or the YELLOW/PURPLE Flip Crayon. Color the crayons at the top of the other pages too. This HWT Flip Crayon uses the primary color yellow with its complementary color purple (made from red and blue). Flipping the crayon to change colors is a fun way to develop coordination and crayon grip.

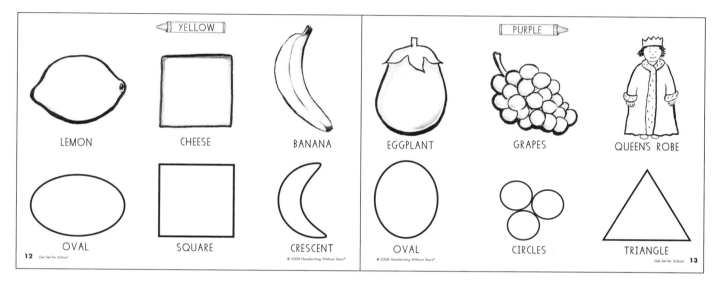

Yellow

Ask about yellow

Can you find the crayon? (Point)
Let's color the crayon yellow.
Do you know anything that is yellow?

Begin to look and learn

Let's find the lemon. (Point)
Let's find the cheese. (Point)
Let's find the banana. (Point)
Let's find the oval. (Point)
Let's find the square. (Point)
Let's find the crescent. (Point)

Color

Color the lemon, cheese, and banana yellow.
Color the shapes below yellow.

Demonstrate

Let's trace shapes. Put finger on shape and trace.

Extra

Point to yellow items in the room.
See who is wearing something yellow.

Purple

Ask about purple

Can you find the crayon? (Point)
Let's color the crayon purple.
Do you know anything that is purple?

Begin to look and learn

Let's find the eggplant. (Point)
Let's find the grapes. (Point)
Let's find the queen's robe. (Point)
Let's find the oval. (Point)
Let's find the circles. (Point)
Let's find the triangle. (Point)

Color

Color the eggplant, grapes, and queen's robe purple.
Color the shapes below purple.

Demonstrate

Show how to color using little circular strokes.

Extra

Point to purple items in the room.
Mix red and blue paint to make purple.
Eat purple grapes for a snack.

Get Started

Help children choose BLUE and ORANGE crayons or the BLUE/ORANGE Flip Crayon. Here's another primary color, BLUE, with its complement ORANGE. When children change colors and pages, it doesn't matter how they flip the crayon. They may use two hands or one.

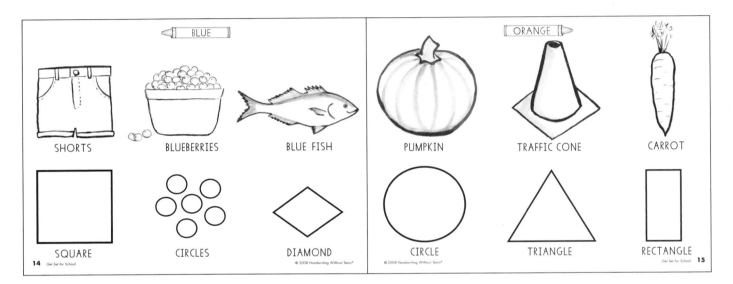

Blue

Ask about blue
Can you find the crayon? (Point)
Let's color the crayon blue.
Do you know anything that is blue?

Begin to look and learn
Let's find the shorts. (Point)
Let's find the blueberries. (Point)
Let's find the fish. (Point)
Let's find the square. (Point)
Let's find the little circles. (Point)
Let's find the diamond. (Point)

Color
Color the shorts, blueberries, and fish blue.
Color the shapes below blue.
Let's sing the *Crayon Song*.
Lyrics and activities for this song are on page 65.

Demonstrate
Show how to color using little circular strokes.

Extra
Point to blue items in the room.
Eat blueberries for a snack.

Orange

Ask about orange
Can you find the crayon? (Point)
Let's color the crayon orange.
Do you know anything that is orange?

Begin to look and learn
Let's find the pumpkin. (Point)
Let's find the traffic cone. (Point)
Let's find the carrot. (Point)
Let's find the circle. (Point)
Let's find the triangle. (Point)
Let's find the rectangle. (Point)

Color
Color the pumpkin, traffic cone, and carrot orange.
Color the shapes below orange.

Demonstrate
Let's trace shapes. Put finger on shape and trace.

Extra
Point to orange items in the room.
Have carrots for a snack.
Mix red and yellow paint to make orange.

Coloring Pages – PINK AND BROWN

Get Started
Help children choose PINK and BROWN crayons or the PINK/BROWN Flip Crayon. This Flip Crayon is ideal for coloring skin tones. The set of 206 Flip Crayons has all the colors children need for this book. You can put out just a few crayons so your students can find ten colors easily. They may skip from page to page, coloring what interests them.

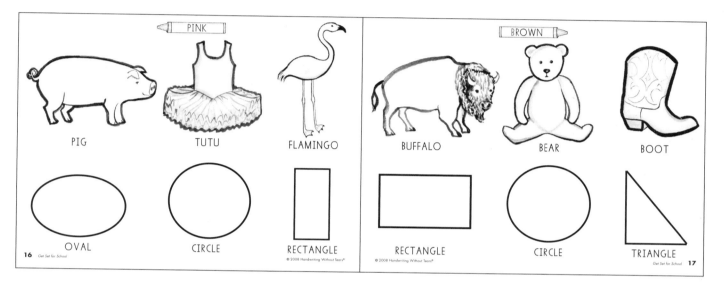

Pink
Ask about pink
Can you find the crayon? (Point)
Let's color the crayon pink.
Do you know anything that is pink?

Begin to look and learn
Let's find the pig. (Point)
Let's find the tutu. (Point)
Let's find the flamingo. (Point)
Let's find the oval. (Point)
Let's find the circle. (Point)
Let's find the rectangle. (Point)

Color
Color the pig, tutu, and flamingo pink.
Color the shapes below pink.

Demonstrate
Let's trace shapes. Put finger on shape and trace.

Extra
Point to pink items in the room.
Make pink by mixing red and white.
Stick out tongues. Notice they're pink.

Brown
Ask about brown
Can you find the crayon? (Point)
Let's color the crayon brown.
Do you know anything that is brown?

Begin to look and learn
Let's find the buffalo. (Point)
Let's find the bear. (Point)
Let's find the boot. (Point)
Let's find the rectangle. (Point)
Let's find the circle. (Point)
Let's find the triangle. (Point)

Color
Color the buffalo, bear, and boot brown.
Color the shapes below brown.

Demonstrate
Let's trace shapes. Put finger on shape and trace.

Extra
Point to brown items in the room.
Mix red and green to make brown.

Get Started

Help children choose GRAY and BLACK crayons or the GRAY/BLACK Flip Crayon. The BLACK crayon is a good choice for tracing letters and numbers, but children may choose any color they like. Teachers like to use GRAY to make their own letters or numbers for children to crayon trace.

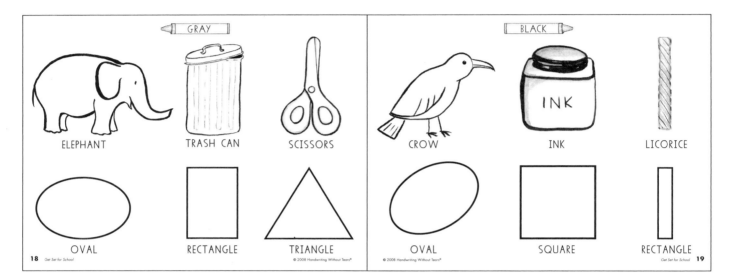

Gray

Ask about gray
Can you find the crayon? (Point)
Let's color the crayon gray.
Do you know anything that is gray?

Begin to look and learn
Let's find the elephant. (Point)
Let's find the trash can. (Point)
Let's find the scissors. (Point)
Let's find the oval. (Point)
Let's find the rectangle. (Point)
Let's find the triangle. (Point)

Color
Color the elephant, trash can, and scissors gray.
Color the shapes below gray.

Demonstrate
Let's trace shapes. Put finger on shape and trace.

Extra
Point to gray items in the room.
Make gray by mixing black and white.

Black

Ask about black
Can you find the crayon? (Point)
Let's color the crayon black.
Do you know anything that is black?

Begin to look and learn
Let's find the crow. (Point)
Let's find the ink. (Point)
Let's find the licorice. (Point)
Let's find the oval. (Point)
Let's find the square. (Point)
Let's find the rectangle. (Point)

Color
Color the crow, ink, and licorice black.
Color the shapes below black.
Let's sing the *Crayon Song*.
Lyrics and activities for this song are on page 65.

Demonstrate
Let's trace shapes. Put finger on shape and trace.

Extra
Point to black items in the room.
See who's wearing black shoes.

Activity Page – MAT MAN™

Get Started Children love singing about, building, and drawing Mat Man. See pages 46-51 or ... the Mat Man activities with your class before using these pages.

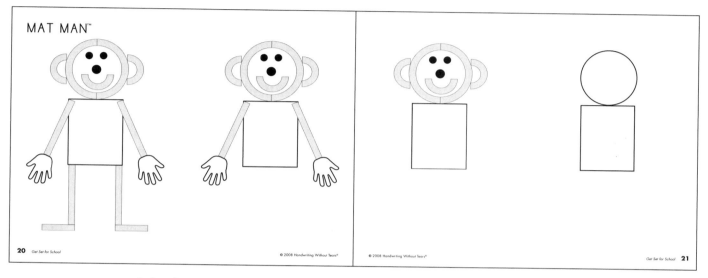

Ask about Mat Man
Do you know Mat Man?
Do you remember the Mat Man song? *Mat Man*, Track 8.
Why do we call him Mat Man? We make him with a mat.

Begin to look and learn
Look at the first Mat Man. Find what's missing from the second, third, and fourth Mat Man.

Color and draw
Color Mat Man's mat and hands blue.
Draw the missing parts as the teacher demonstrates.

Demonstrate Mat Man
At the board - Teacher draws the complete Mat Man.
1. Erase his legs and feet.
   Ask   What does he need? Let's draw legs like this.
2. Erase his arms and hands, legs and feet.
   Ask   What does he need? Let's draw arms and hands, legs and feet like this.
3. Erase Mat Man and draw just a circle and mat.
   Ask   What does he need? Let's draw.

Extra
Demonstrate adding extra parts or clothing the children want.
Read the *MAT MAN SHAPES* book.

Fun Focus
You can make other Mat People or Mat Animals.
Use a triangle as a dress for Mat Lady.

VERTICAL AND HORIZONTAL

Get Started These pages give experience with vertical and horizontal lines. Verticals are made with down strokes. Horizontals are made like this →for right-handed children and like this ← for left-handed children.

Ask about the chicks and legs
How many chicks do you see?
How many legs does a chick have?
How many legs do you have?

Begin to look and learn
The fence has posts and rails.
The posts go down into the dirt.
The rails go across, from post to post.

Color and draw
Color the fence. (Use vertical and horizontal strokes)
Color the grass. (Use short down strokes.)
Color the chicks.

Demonstrate tracing down
Let's trace the chicks' two legs:
Down, stop; down, stop.

Extra
Use the *Get Set for School Sing Along* CD, *Bird Legs*, Track 12.

Ask about the ducks
How many ducks do you see?
How many legs do ducks have?
How many wings? Eyes?

Begin to look and learn
Who's sitting on the fence?
What are the parts of a fence? Posts and rails.
What are the ducks standing in? A puddle.

Color and draw
Color the fence, grass, and ducks.
Color the puddle blue.
Color the sky on both pages blue.

Demonstrate tracing down
Let's trace the ducks two legs:
Down, stop; down, stop.

Teach

BIG LINE   + LITTLE LINE

Get Started Prepare children for **L** by drawing a cross. Developmentally, the cross is taught after the circle. However, because we are teaching a letter with horizontal/vertical strokes, we teach cross now. Demonstrate cross for students. Have students put their crayons on the arrow. Say "Big line down, big line across. Look, we made a cross." Allow children to choose which picture they would like to make in the final spot. Children who are not ready for crayon tracing can finger trace over each cross. It's fine if a child doesn't cross exactly in the middle. Have students look for the lizard on the cross page. (It's on the window sill.)

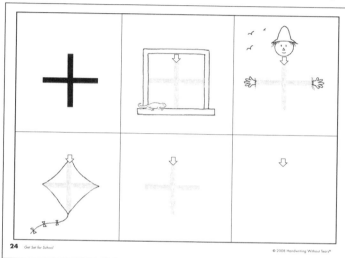 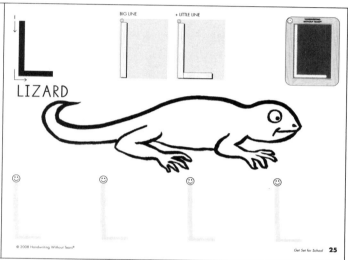

Ask about L
Do you know: **L** words? **L** names? **L** sounds? Have you ever seen a lizard?

Begin to look and learn
This is the **L** page. Let's find **L**s on this page. (Point)
Look. There's a lizard. (Point)
Lizard starts with **L**.
Is a lizard an animal or a person? Where do lizards live?
What do lizards have? What color(s) are lizards? (Show pictures.)

Color and draw
Let's color the lizard. (Show different ways to color.)
What about adding spots or stripes? Rocks or grass for the lizard? (Demonstrate.)
The lizard needs a tongue!

Demonstrate tracing L
Let's write **L** for lizard. Put the crayon on the ☺.
Big line down. Little line across.

Extra
Stick tongue out like a lizard. Move it up and down and side to side.

Fun focus
Talk about in and out. Is the lizard's tongue in or out?
Note: Make up verses for cross like those on track 17.

GET SET FOR SCHOOL
Sing Along

17

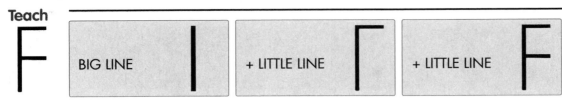

F

| BIG LINE | ⌐ + LITTLE LINE | + LITTLE LINE |

Get Started

Developmentally, the square is taught after the cross. This shape contains vertical and horizontal strokes. Demonstrate square for the students. Have students put their crayons on the arrow. Say "big line down, big line across the bottom, big line up, big line across the top. Look, we made a square." Use *My Teacher Draws*, Track 17, to teach simple shape drawing. Allow children to choose which picture they would like to make in the final spot. Children who are not ready for crayon tracing can finger trace over each square.

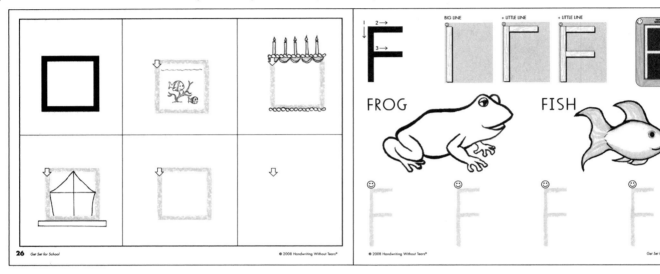

Ask about F
Do you know: **F** words? **F** names? **F** sounds? **F** months?
Have you seen a frog or a fish?

Begin to look and learn
This is the **F** page. Let's find the **F**s. (Point)
Look. There's a frog and a fish. (Point)
Frog and fish start with **F**.
Talk about: how they move, where they live, 4 legs and no legs, 1 tail, fins.

Color and draw
Color the frog and fish. (Show different ways to color.)
What about adding water and grass?

Demonstrate tracing F
Let's write **F**. Put the crayon on the ☺.
Big line down. Jump to the ☺. Little line across the top.
Little line across the middle.

Extra
Cup one hand. Hold the other hand in a fist and pretend it's a frog jumping on the other hand. Jump like a frog with large movements around the classroom.

Fun focus
Swim around the room like a fish. Jump like a frog.

Teach

| BIG LINE | + LITTLE LINE | + LITTLE LINE | + LITTLE LINE |

 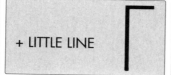 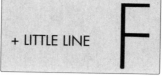 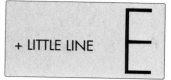

Get Started

Prepare children for **E** with this pre-stroke page. This page has horizontal lines for tracing. Developmentally, the horizontal line is taught after the vertical line and is one of the easiest strokes for a child. Demonstrate horizontal lines for students. Have them put their crayons on the arrow. Say "big line across. Stop. Look, we made a line." Children who are not ready for crayon tracing can finger trace over each line. It's fine if a child makes the line a little too long. With practice, they will learn to stop with more control. Color the page.

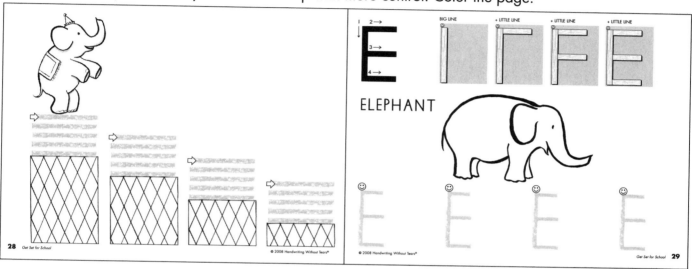

Ask about E

Do you know: **E** words? **E** names? **E** sounds? Have you seen an elephant?

Begin to look and learn

This is the **E** page. Let's find the **E**s. (Point)
Look. There's an elephant. (Point)
Elephant starts with **E**.
Talk about: body parts, nose/trunk and how it's used, big ears, 4 legs, 1 tail, elephant size, sound, where elephants live.

Color and draw

Remind children about using a good crayon grip by singing the *Crayon Song*, Track 5, *Get Set for School Sing Along* CD.
Color elephant gray. What about adding peanuts, trees, and grass?

Demonstrate tracing E

Let's write **E**. Put the crayon on the ☺.
Big line down. Jump to the ☺. Little line across the top, middle, and bottom.

Extra

Bend over, put hands together, use arms as a trunk and swing side to side.

Fun focus

Compare heavy and light.

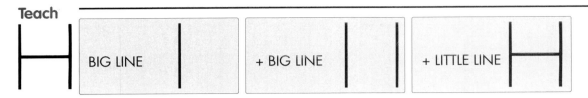

| BIG LINE | + BIG LINE | + LITTLE LINE |

Get Started Rectangles use vertical and horizontal lines. Demonstrate rectangle for the students. Have them put their crayons on the arrow. Say, "little line down, big line across the bottom, little line up, big line across the top. Look, we made a rectangle." Allow children to choose which picture they would like to make in the final spot. Children who are not ready for crayon tracing may finger trace over each rectangle. Have students look for the house on the rectangle page.

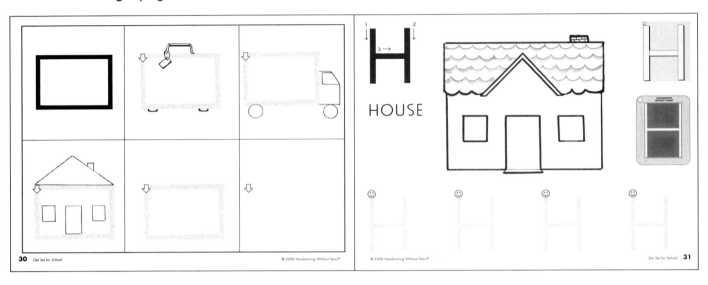

Ask about H
Do you know: **H** words? **H** names? **H** sounds?
Have you seen a house? Who lives in a house? Does your house have a chimney?
What does the chimney do?

Begin to look and learn
This is the **H** page. Let's find the **H**s. (Point)
Look. There's a house. (Point)
House starts with **H**.
Talk about: 1 house, 1 door, 1 chimney, 2 windows.

Color and draw
Sing the *Crayon Song* (see page 65). Color the house any color.
What about adding grass, doorknob, smoke from chimney, window panes?

Demonstrate tracing H
Let's trace **H**. Put the crayon on the ☺.
Big line down. Big line down. Little line across.

Extra
Tell the story of the Three Little Pigs.

Fun focus
Make a house out of a cardboard box.

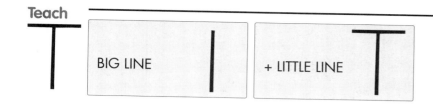

T

BIG LINE	+ LITTLE LINE

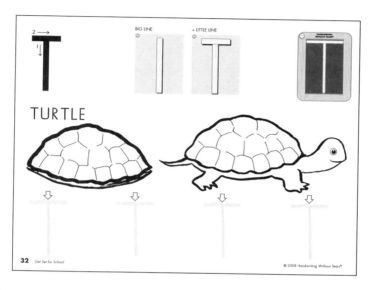

TURTLE

Ask about T
Do you know: **T** words? **T** names? **T** sounds? **T** days?
Have you seen a turtle?

Begin to look and learn
This is the **T** page. Let's find the **T**s. (Point)
Look. There's a turtle. (Point)
Turtle starts with **T**.
Talk about: opposites (in/out, hard/soft), where turtles live, 4 legs, how turtles hide in their shell, swim in water.

Color and draw
Sing the *Crayon Song* (see page 65).
Color the turtle brown or green.
What about adding water, a sun, rocks?

Demonstrate tracing T
Let's write **T**. Put the crayon on the ⬇.
Big line down.
Little line across top.

Extra
Make turtles as a craft project.

Fun focus
Make **T** for Time Out with your hands, just like a referee.

| BIG LINE | + LITTLE LINE | + LITTLE LINE |

Get Started Remind children about *The Ant, The Bug and The Bee.*

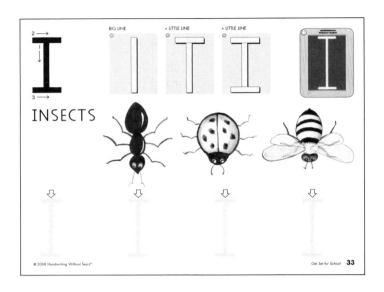

Ask about I
Do you know: **I** words? **I** names? **I** sounds?
Have you seen insects?

Begin to look and learn
This is the **I** page. Let's find the **I**s. (Point)
Look. There are insects. (Point)
Insects start with **I**.
Talk about: where insects live, 6 legs, 2 antenna,
wings to fly, another name for insects, size.

Color and draw
Color the ladybug red and the bee yellow.
What about drawing another insect or bug?

Demonstrate tracing I
Let's write **I**. Put the crayon on the ⇩.
Big line down.
Little line across the top and little line across the bottom.

Extra
Fly around like insects.
Sing *The Ant, The Bug and The Bee*, Track 14.

U

BIG LINE	I
+ TURN	L
+ BIG LINE	U

Get Started

This is a page for coloring that goes along with the *Rain Song*, Track 24, on the *Get Set for School Sing Along* CD. Children enjoy finding the pictures at the top of the big picture.

RAIN   PUDDLE   RAINCOAT   BOOTS   BOAT   RAINHAT

34 *Get Set for School*   © 2008 Handwriting Without Tears®

U

UMBRELLA

© 2008 Handwriting Without Tears®   *Get Set for School* 35

Ask about U
Do you know: **U** words? **U** names? **U** sounds?
Have you used an umbrella?

Begin to look and learn
This is the **U** page. Let's find the **U**s. (Point)
Look. There's an umbrella. (Point)
Umbrella starts with **U**.
Talk about opposites: open/shut, up/down, wet/dry.

Color and draw
Color the umbrella. What about using different colors for each section of the umbrella?

Demonstrate tracing U
Let's trace **U**. Put the crayon on the ☺.
Big line down.
Turn and go across the bottom.
Big line up.

Extra
Make an umbrella, raincoat, and boots for Mat Man.

Fun focus
Use toy cars and make **U** turns.

GET SET FOR SCHOOL
Sing Along

24

MAGIC C

Making C strokes prepare children for drawing circles and writing. Children may have made circular scribbles by starting anywhere and just going round and round. Now it's time for you, the Magic C Bunny, and the *Magic C* song, (Track 6, *Get Set for School Sing Along* CD) to teach them how to start:

- Circles
- Letters—**C O Q G S**

This habit is important now and will be even more important in kindergarten when children learn the lowercase letters that start with a Magic c stroke: **a**, **d**, **g**, **o** and **q**.

Play *Magic C Bunny Says*....

Play *Simon Says* as *Magic C Bunny Says*. Have the puppet whisper in your ear when you say, "Magic C Bunny Says." Other times, just give the direction without the puppet whispering in your ear and without saying, "Magic C Bunny Says." Children should follow only when you say, "Magic C Bunny Says."

Make Your Own Magic C Bunnies

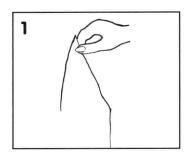

1 Open paper napkin. Hold by one corner.

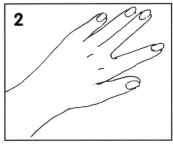

2 Spread index and middle fingers apart.

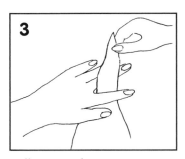

3 Pull corner between your index and middle fingers. (First ear)

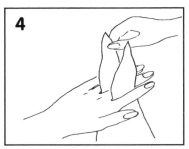

4 Take the next corner. Pull corner between your middle and ring fingers. (Second ear)

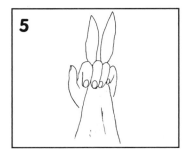

5 Fold fingers into palm.

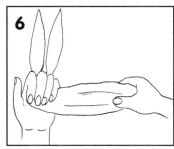

6 Pull napkin out to side.

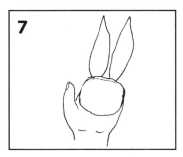

7 Wrap napkin over fingers and tuck into hand.

8 Add the face with a pen. It's a bunny! You may slip the bunny off your fingers and give it to a child. Tape or staple the napkin to hold it.

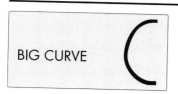

BIG CURVE

Get Started

Prepare children for **C** with this pre-stroke page. Use the Magic C Bunny puppet to help you teach. Demonstrate Magic Cs for students. Have them put their crayons on the arrow. Say "Magic C Bunny wants us to make a Magic C to help get his car to the stop sign. Magic C. Stop. Look, we made a Magic C." Make car sounds while tracing the stroke. Use the *Get Set for School Sing Along* CD, Track 6, to teach Magic C. Children who are not ready for crayon tracing can finger trace over each Magic C. Color the page.

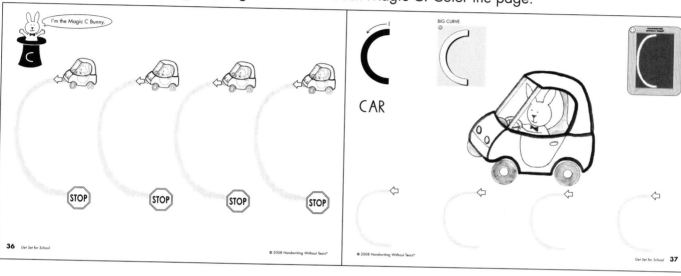

Ask about C

Do you know: **C** words? **C** names? **C** sounds?
Have you ever seen a car like this one?

Begin to look and learn

This is the **C** page. Let's find **C**s on this page. (Point)
Look. There's a car. (Point)
Car starts with **C**.
Is a car alive? Is it an animal, a person, or a thing? What do cars do? What do cars have? What color cars have you seen? (Show pictures.)

Color and draw

Let's color the car. (Show different ways to color.)
Any designs? Does your car need a road? (Demonstrate.)

Demonstrate tracing C

Let's write **C** for car. Put the crayon on the ⇦. Big curve. Stop at the bottom.
Sing the *Magic C* song, Track 6 on the *Get Set for School Sing Along* CD.

Extra

Curve left hand to make **C**. Use right index finger to trace **C**.

Fun focus

Use the Magic C Bunny puppet to introduce **C** or make your own.

Note: *Get Set for School* uses pictures and ☺ or ⇦ icons to help children start shapes and letters correctly.

BIG CURVE	+ BIG CURVE

Get Started

Prepare children for **O** with this pre-stroke page. This page has water in the shape of an **O** for tracing. Demonstrate the **O** stroke for students. Have students put their crayons on the arrow. Say, "Magic C. Keep going. Stop at the top. Look we traced an **O**." Children who are not yet ready for crayon tracing can finger trace around the circle of water. Encourage the child to go around more than once. Color the page.

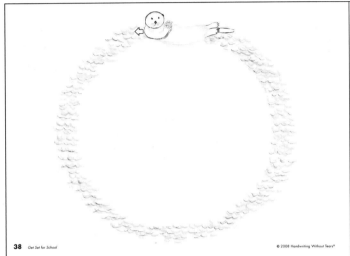

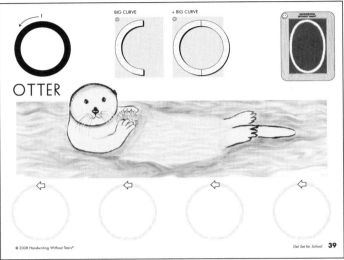

Ask about O
Do you know: **O** words? **O** names? **O** months? **O** sounds?
Have you seen an otter?

Begin to look and learn
This is the **O** page. Let's find the **O**s. (Point)
Look. There's an otter. (Point)
Otter starts with **O**.
Talk about: where the otter lives, what he's doing,
shape of head, floating on back.

Color and draw
Color the otter and the water.

Demonstrate tracing O
Let's write **O**. Put the crayon on the ⇦.
Magic C. Keep going. Stop at the top.

Extra
Have Cheerios® or round pretzels for a snack.

Fun focus
Make **O**s with Wood Pieces first. See page 41.

 **BIG CURVE**
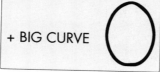 **+ BIG CURVE**
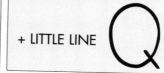 **+ LITTLE LINE**

Get Started

Prepare children for **Q** by drawing a circle. Developmentally, the circle is taught after the horizontal line. Demonstrate circle for the students. Have them put their crayons on the arrow. Say "Magic C. Keep going. Look we made a circle." Use the *Get Set for School Sing Along* CD (Track 6 or 17) to teach simple drawings using circle. Allow children to choose which picture they would like to make in the final spot. Children who are not ready for crayon tracing can finger trace over each circle.

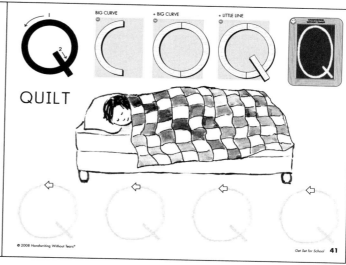

Ask about Q

Do you know: **Q** words? **Q** names? **Q** sounds?
Have you seen a quilt?

Begin to look and learn

This is the **Q** page. Let's find the **Q**s. (Point)
Look. There's a quilt. (Point)
Quilt starts with **Q**.
Talk about how quilts: keep us warm, are made of pieces, have lots of colors.

Color and draw

Color the quilt. Use many colors to aim and scribble on the squares.

Demonstrate tracing Q

Let's write **Q**. Put the crayon on the ⇦.
Magic C. Keep going. Stop at the top. Add a little line.

Extra

Act like ducks and say QUACK, QUACK, QUACK.
Then say QUIET and stop. Repeat.

Fun focus

Bring in quilts or blankets. Have children get under a quilt and be quiet.

 BIG CURVE

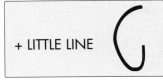 + LITTLE LINE

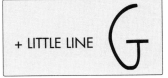 + LITTLE LINE

Get Started

Get ready for **G** by cutting the grass. Demonstrate the formation of **G**. Have students put their crayons on the arrow. Say, "Magic C, little line up, little line across. Look, we traced **G**." Make mowing sounds as you trace. Children who are not ready for crayon tracing can finger trace. Color the page.

Ask about G

Do you know: **G** words? **G** names? **G** sounds?
(Note: **G** sounds like **J** in George/gym/gentle.)
Have you seen a grasshopper?

Begin to look and learn

This is the **G** Page. Let's find the **G**s. (Point)
Look. There's a grasshopper in the grass. (Point)
They start with **G**.
Talk about: insects, 6 legs with 2 big ones for hopping, cutting grass.

Color and draw

Color using two shades of green.
What about adding a bug or a worm in the grass?

Demonstrate tracing G

Let's write **G**. Put the crayon on the ⇦.
Magic C. Little line up. Little line across.

Extra

Hop like grasshoppers.
Make cuts on green paper to make grass.

Fun focus

Wear green. Eat green snacks.

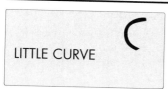

LITTLE CURVE

+ LITTLE CURVE

Get Started

Prepare children for **S** with this pre-stroke page. This page has little curves and curves in the shape of an **S** for tracing. Demonstrate little curves. Have students put their crayons on the arrow. Say "Little curve. Stop. Look, we made a little curve." Demonstrate skating the other way. Now make the snowboarding squirrel and child ride down with an **S** curve. Children who are not ready for crayon tracing can finger trace over the curves. It's fine if a child does not stop exactly at the end of the stroke. With practice, they will learn to stop. Color the page.

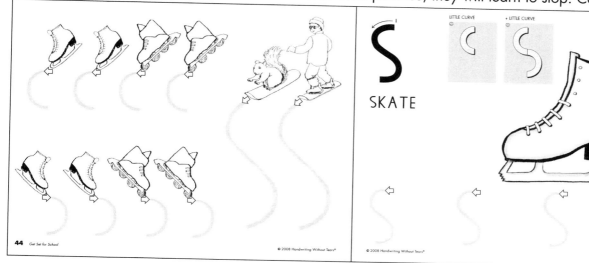

Ask about S
Do you know: **S** words? **S** names? **S** sounds? **S** days? **S** month?
Have you seen a skate?

Begin to look and learn
This is the **S** page. Let's find the **S**s. (Point)
Look. There's a skate. (Point)
Skate starts with **S**.
Talk about: places you can skate, who has skates, if they have seen anyone skate.

Color and draw
Color the skate.

Demonstrate tracing S
Let's write **S**. Put the crayon on the ⇦.
Make a little Magic c curve. Make a little curve the other way.

Extra
Children can make a dough snake into an **S**.

Fun focus
Children can pretend that they are skating around the room.

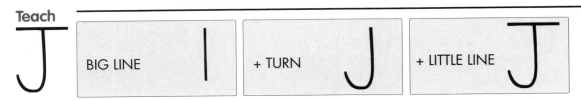

| BIG LINE | + TURN | + LITTLE LINE |

Get Started

Prepare for **J** by pretend skating. Demonstrate the **J** turn for students. Say, "Big line down. Turn. Stop." Demonstrate little lines. Have students put their crayons on the arrow. Say "Little line across. Stop." Children who are not ready for crayon tracing can finger trace. It's fine if a child makes the line a little too long at first. With practice, they will learn to stop. Color the page.

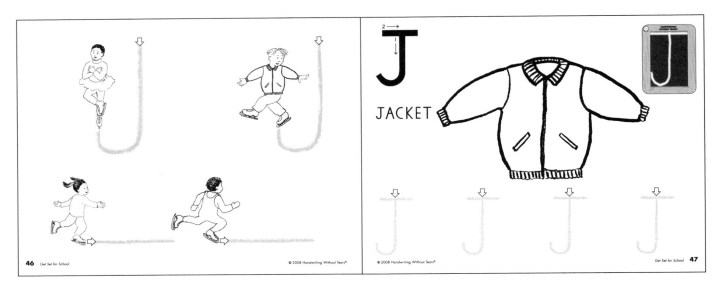

Ask about J

Do you know: **J** words? **J** names? **J** sounds? **J** months? Do you have a jacket?

Begin to look and learn

This is the **J** page. Let's find the **J**s. (Point)
Look. There's a jacket. (Point)
Jacket starts with **J**.
Talk about: January and June weather, hanging up jackets, parts of a jacket, and how many sleeves.

Color and draw

Color the jacket.

Demonstrate tracing J

Let's write **J**. Put the crayon on the ⇩.
Big line down. Turn. Little line across the top.

Extra

J is for jumping too. Jump around the room.
J is for jogging. Jog around the room.

Fun focus

Practice putting on and taking off jackets. Practice zipping or buttoning.
Teach up/down, on/off, and open/closed concepts.
Make a jacket for Mat Man.

BIG & LITTLE CURVES

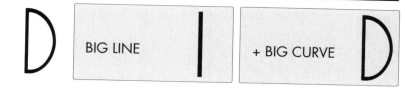

Get Started

Prepare children for **D P B** and **R** with this pre-stroke page. Demonstrate big curves using the big ducks. Have students put their crayons on the arrow. Say "Big curve. Stop. Look, we made a big curve." Teach little curves with the little ducks. Quack like ducks as you're making the strokes. Children who are not ready for crayon tracing can finger trace. Initially, it's fine if a child doesn't stop at the end of the curve. With practice, they will learn to stop. Color the page.

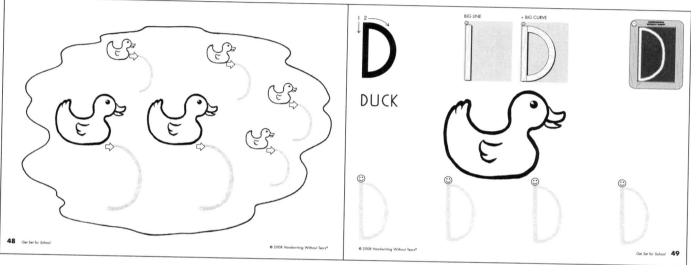

Ask about D

Do you know: **D** words? **D** months? **D** names? **D** sounds?
Have you ever seen a duck?

Begin to look and learn

This is the **D** page. Let's find **D**s on this page. (Point)
Look. There's a duck. (Point)
Duck starts with **D**.
Is a duck an animal or a person?
Where do ducks live? What do ducks have? What color are ducks? (Show pictures.)

Color and draw

Let's color the duck. (Show different ways to color.)

Demonstrate tracing D

Let's write **D**. Put the crayon on the ☺.
Big line down. Jump back to ☺. Big curve to the bottom.

Extra

Make duck sounds. Fly or walk like ducks.

Fun focus

Float a rubber ducky. Play with sinking and floating things.

P

| BIG LINE | I | + LITTLE CURVE | P |

Ask about P
Do you know: **P** words? **P** names? **P** sounds?
Have you seen a pail?

Begin to look and learn
This is the **P** page. Let's find the **P**s. (Point)
Look. There's a pail. (Point)
Pail starts with **P**.
Talk about: how pails are used, what goes in them,
Jack and Jill Nursery Rhyme.

Color and draw
Color the pail. What about putting something in it?

Demonstrate tracing P
Let's write **P**. Put the crayon on the ☺.
Big line down. Jump to the ☺.
Little curve to the middle.

Extra
Make a bucket brigade and pass the pail like firefighters did long ago.

Fun focus
Teach in/out by placing things in pails.
P is for Peppermint. Smell peppermint.

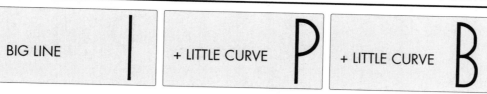

| B | BIG LINE | I | + LITTLE CURVE | P | + LITTLE CURVE | B |

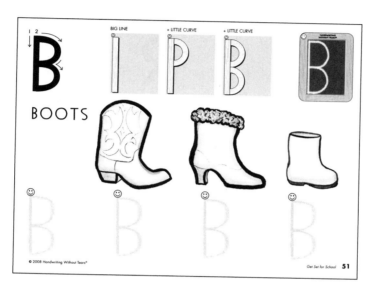

Ask about B
Do you know: **B** words? **B** names? **B** sounds?
Do you have boots?

Begin to look and learn
This is the **B** page. Let's find the **B**s. (Point)
Look. There are three boots. (Point)
Boot starts with **B**.
Talk about: different purpose boots, baby booties, big/little boots.

Color and draw
Color the boots any color.
What about adding mud, puddle, grass? (Demonstrate.)

Demonstrate tracing B
Let's write **B**. Put the crayon on the ☺.
Big line down. Jump to the ☺.
Little curve to the middle. Little curve to the bottom.

Extra
B is for ball.
Sort balls by color, type, and size.

Fun focus
Talk about cowboy boots and pretend to ride horses.

DIAGONALS

R | BIG LINE | I | + LITTLE CURVE | P | + LITTLE LINE | R

Get Started

Prepare children for the diagonal in **R** with this pre-stroke page. Diagonal lines are the most difficult. Have students put their crayons on the arrow. Say, "Slide down the rake handle. Stop." Children who are not ready for crayon tracing can finger trace over each line. Color the page. Add leaves on the ground.

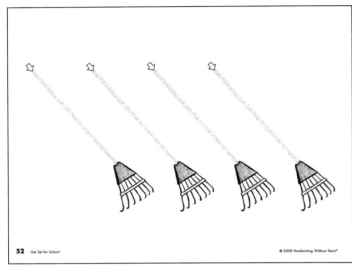

Ask about R

Do you know: **R** words? **R** names? **R** sounds?
Have you seen a rake? Have you ever used a rake? What do rakes do?

Begin to look and learn

This is the **R** page. Let's find the **R**s. (Point)
Look. There's a rake. (Point)
Rake starts with **R**.
Talk about: 1 handle.

Color and draw

Color rake any color.
What about adding leaves, grass? (Demonstrate.)

Demonstrate tracing R

Let's trace **R**. Put the crayon on the ☺.
Big line down. Jump to the ☺. Little curve to the middle.
Little line to the corner.

Extra

Rake leaves. Use a rake to make patterns in a sandbox. **R** is for run.
Go outside and run.

Fun focus

Find everything that is red in the room. Who's wearing red?

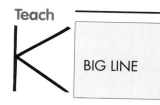

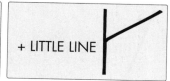

BIG LINE | + LITTLE LINE | + LITTLE LINE

Get Started

Prepare children for **K** with this pre-stroke page. This page has little diagonal lines for tracing. Because the stroke begins at the kite and ends at the child's hand, it gives children practice with the ability to start/stop. Have students put their crayons on the arrow. Say, "Slide down the kite string to the hands." Make noises like the wind as you're making the strokes. Children who are not ready for crayon tracing can finger trace over each line. Color the page. Use different color crayons.

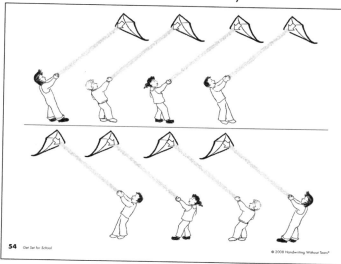

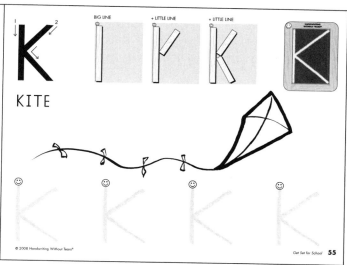

Ask about K

Do you know: **K** words? **K** names? **K** sounds?
Have you flown a kite?

Begin to look and learn

This is the **K** page. Let's find the **K**s. (Point)
Look. There's a kite. (Point)
Kite starts with **K**.
Talk about: wind, different types of kites.

Color and draw

Color the kites any color.

Demonstrate tracing K

Let's write **K**. Put the crayon on the ☺.
Big line down. Jump to the other corner.
Little line slides to the middle, little line slides to the bottom.

Extra

Make kites. Wind string.

Fun focus

Pretend to give the **K** a karate kick when making the letter.

A | BIG LINE  | + BIG LINE  | + LITTLE LINE

Get Started

The first letter of the alphabet is one of the most difficult. Often, children mistakenly start at the bottom. That's why the pre-stroke page is so important. Demonstrate starting at the top where the alligators are. Put the crayon on the arrow, say, "Big line slides down. Stop." Make noises like the alligator is eating the crayon stroke "chomp, chomp, chomp" as you're making the strokes. Color the alligators. Use different crayons to make each stroke. This also gives practice with picking up and holding a crayon correctly.

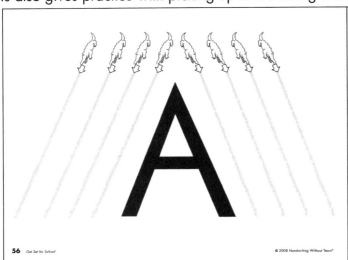

Ask about A

Do you know: **A** words? **A** names? **A** sounds? **A** months?
Have you seen an alligator?

Begin to look and learn

This is the **A** page. Let's find the **A**s. (Point)
Look. There's an alligator. (Point)
Alligator starts with **A**.
Talk about: where alligators live, 1 tail, lots of teeth, 4 legs.

Color and draw

Color the alligator green.
What about adding water, a sun, rocks. (Demonstrate.)

Demonstrate tracing A

Let's write **A**. Put the crayon on the ✍.
Big line slides down. Jump back to the top.
Big line slides down. Little line across.

Extra

Crawl on the floor like alligators. Make hand shadow alligator mouths.

Fun focus

A is for apple. Sort apples by color and size.

Shape Page – TRIANGLE AND DIAMOND

Developmentally, the triangle and diamond come after the circle and square. Motor experiences with slides, ramps, cones, and funnels make diagonal lines and these shapes easier for children.

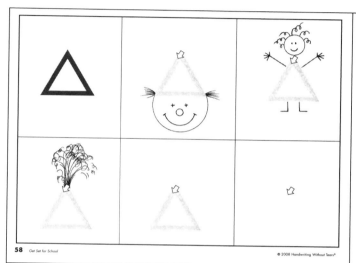 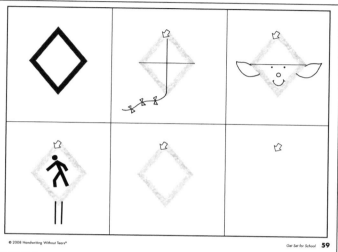

Ask about the triangle
How many sides does the triangle have?
How many points/angles do you see?

Begin to look and learn
A triangle can be a hat.
A triangle can be a dress.
A triangle can be a volcano.
What else could a triangle be?
(ice cream cone, warning sign, tree, etc.)

Color
Color the triangle and pictures.

Demonstrate for tracing and copying
Watch me draw a triangle.
1. Big line slides down.
2. Big line goes across.
3. Big line slides up to the top.
Children trace and copy the triangles.
They turn the last triangles into pictures.

Extra
Play *My Teacher Draws* song, Track 17, from the *Get Set for School Sing Along* CD.

Ask about the diamond
How many sides does the diamond have?
How many points/angles does it have?

Begin to look and learn
A diamond can be a kite.
A diamond can be a face/hat for an elf.
A diamond can be a road sign.

Color
Color the diamond and pictures.

Demonstrate for tracing and copying
Watch me make a big diamond in the air.
Follow me as I make the diamond
1. Big line slides down to the side.
2. Big line slides down to the bottom.
3. Big line slides up to the side.
4. Big line slides up to the top.
Watch me write a diamond (same way)
Children trace and copy the diamonds.
They turn the last triangles into pictures.

Extra
Play *My Teacher Draws* song, Track 17, from the *Get Set for School Sing Along* CD.

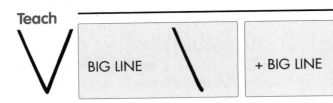

BIG LINE	+ BIG LINE

Get Started

Prepare children for **V** and **W** with this pre-stroke page. This page has a roller coaster in the shape of a **V**. Demonstrate big line slides down, big line slides up. Have students put their crayons on the arrow. Say "Big line slides down, big line slides up. Look, we moved like a **V**." Allow children to make noises as if they are on a roller coaster while making the strokes. They can practice making diagonal strokes on the structure of the roller coaster. Color the page.

Ask about V

Do you know: **V** words? **V** names? **V** sounds?
Have you been in a van?

Begin to look and learn

This is the **V** page. Let's find **V**s on this page. (Point)
Look. There's a van. (Point)
Van starts with **V**.
What do vans do? What color/s are vans? (Show pictures.)

Color and draw

Let's color the van. (Show different ways to color.)
Draw people in the van.

Demonstrate tracing V

Let's write **V** for van. Put the crayon on the ☺.
Big line slides down. Big line slides up.

Extra

Make fingers into **V**s.

Fun focus

Make **V** with wood pieces.

M	I BIG LINE	+ BIG LINE Λ	+ BIG LINE Λ

Get Started

Prepare children for **M** with this pre-stroke page. The mice are looking for cheese. Demonstrate big line down. Have students put their crayons on the arrow by the first mouse. Say "Big line down. Stop. Now put the crayon on the next arrow. Big line slides down, big line slides up, big line down. Look, it looks like **M**." Make sniffing sounds while making the strokes. Encourage children to trace more than once with different colors. By using more than one color, children get practice picking up and holding their crayons.

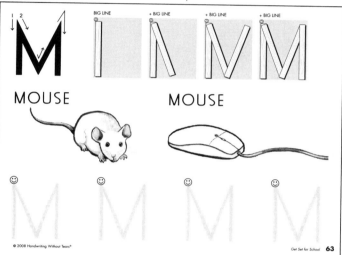

MOUSE   MOUSE

Ask about M

Do you know: **M** words? **M** names? **M** sounds? **M** months? **M** day?
Have you seen a mouse?

Begin to look and learn

This is the **M** page. Let's find the **M**s. (Point)
Look. There's a mouse. Look, there's a different mouse (a computer mouse). (Point)
Mouse starts with **M**.
Talk about mice: their size, where they live, what they eat.

Color and draw

Color both mice. What about adding cheese?

Demonstrate tracing M

Let's trace **M**. Put the crayon on the ☺.
Big line down. Jump to the ☺. Big line slides down. And up. And down.

Extra

Three Blind Mice Nursery Rhyme.

Fun focus

M is for Middle.
Play with Mat Man and put a belly button in the middle of his body.

Get Started

Prepare children for **N** with this pre-stroke page. This page has nozzles squirting water vertically and diagonally. Demonstrate big lines down, big lines diagonally, and big lines up. Have students put their crayons on the arrow. Say "Big line down, big line slides down, big line up. Look, we moved like **N**." Use a blue crayon for water. Color the nozzles.

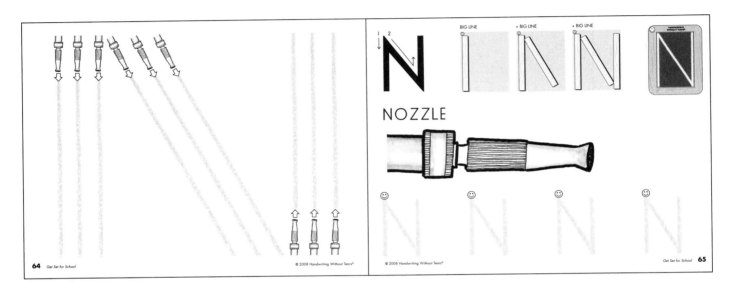

Ask about N

Do you know: **N** words? **N** names? **N** sounds?
Have you seen water squirted out of a nozzle?

Begin to look and learn

This is the **N** page. Let's find the **N**s. (Point)
Look. There's a nozzle. (Point)
Nozzle starts with **N**.
Talk about: what nozzles do, what comes out of a nozzle,
on/off concepts, what you can water.

Color and draw

Color the nozzle. Draw water squirting out of the nozzle.

Demonstrate tracing N

Let's write **N**. Put the crayon on the ☺.
Big line down. Jump to the ☺. Big line slides down. Big line goes up.

Extra

N is for no. Shake head for no. Nod head for yes.
Play with hose and nozzle. Squirt water.

Fun focus

N is for noise. Make car, truck, and airplane noises.

Shapes Review

Here are two shape pages. The first is a review of basic shapes, presented in developmental order. The next is taken from the *MAT MAN SHAPES* book. In that book, Mat Man has his usual mat, a rectangle; and then we give him different shapes. This page shows Mat Man with four shapes: rectangle, oval, diamond, and heart. Use each page by itself and then go back to look at them together. Encourage children to name, discuss, and compare the different shapes.

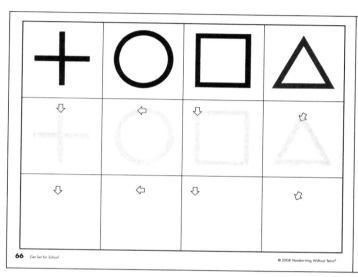
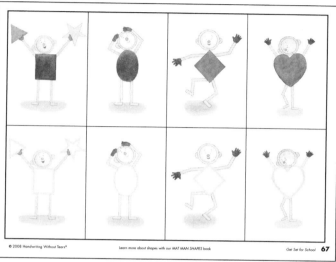

Cross, Circle, Square, Triangle

Ask about the shapes
Where is the circle? (Point)
Where is the triangle? (Point)
Where is the cross? (Point)
Where is the circle? (Point)

Begin to look and learn
The cross has two lines.
The circle has an inside and outside.
The square has 4 sides and 4 corners.
The triangle has 3 sides and 3 angles.

Color
Color the circle, square, and triangle at the top.

Demonstrate for tracing and copying
Watch me draw the shapes. Trace and copy like me.
Cross: down and across. Circle: Start with a Magic C .
Go around to the top.
Square: Down, across, up, across
Triangle: Down, across, up

Extra
Children may color the completed shapes.
They may make faces in the circles.

MAT MAN SHAPES

Ask about Mat Man™
Can you find Mat Man with a heart shape? (Point)
Can you find him with an oval body?
Can you find him with a diamond body?
Where is the real Mat Man and what is he holding?

Begin to look and learn
Let's find the real Mat Man (Point)
His body is a Mat, a rectangle.
Compare square and rectangle.
Compare circle and oval.
Compare square and diamond. (angle)

Color
Color the shapes.

Demonstrate
Draw Mat Man with a different shape,
perhaps making Mat Lady with a triangle.
Have children imitate on a separate paper.

Extra
These illustrations are from the *MAT MAN SHAPES* book. If you have this book, read it to your students and try the suggested activities.

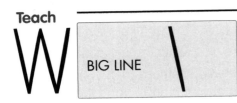

BIG LINE	+ BIG LINE	+ BIG LINE	+ BIG LINE
\	V	W	W

Ask about W
Do you know: **W** words? **W** names? **W** sounds? **W** day?
Have you seen a wagon?

Begin to look and learn
This is the **W** page. Let's find the **W**s. (Point)
Look. There's an a wagon and a wheel. (Point)
Wagon and wheel start with **W**.
Talk about: opposites (in/out, push/pull, on/off, empty/full) riding in a wagon,
how wheels work.

Color and draw
Color wagon red and wheels black.
What about adding grass, rocks, dirt, or a person riding in the wagon?

Demonstrate tracing W
Let's trace **W**. Put the crayon on the ☺.
Big line slides down. And up. And down. And up.

Extra
Make covered wagons out of cardboard boxes.
Count wheels on bikes, tricycles, and cars.
Make cars slide down ramps.

Fun focus
W is for white and winter. Use a Q–Tip® to dab white snow spots on blue paper.

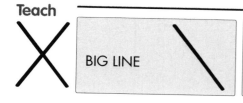

| BIG LINE |  | + BIG LINE | X |

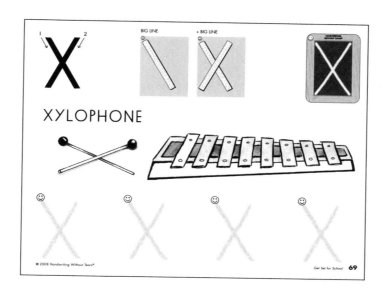

Ask about X
Do you know: **X** words? **X** names? **X** sounds?
Have you seen a xylophone?

Begin to look and learn
This is the **X** page. Let's find the **X**s. (Point)
Look. There's a xylophone. (Point)
Xylophone starts with **X**, but it doesn't make an **X** sound.
Talk about: what a xylophone is and how it is played.

Color and draw
Color the xylophone.

Demonstrate tracing X
Let's write **X**. Put the crayon on the ☺.
Big line down. Jump to the top of the other big line.
Big line down.

Extra
Play a xylophone. Make **X** with two big lines.

Fun focus
Find EXIT signs. Play trains. Make a railroad crossing sign.

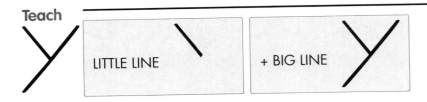

LITTLE LINE	+ BIG LINE

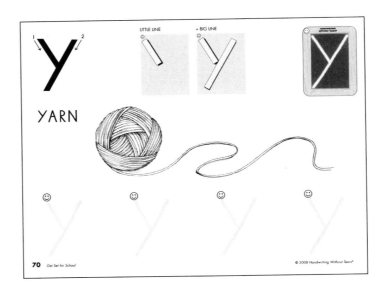

Ask about Y
Do you know: **Y** words? **Y** names? **Y** sounds?
Have you seen yarn?

Begin to look and learn
This is the **Y** page. Let's find the **Y**s. (Point)
Look. There's yarn. (Point)
Yarn starts with **Y**.
Talk about: the shape (round), what it's used for, color, long/short.

Color and draw
Color the yarn yellow.

Demonstrate tracing Y
Let's trace **Y**. Put the crayon on the ☺.
Little line slides down to the middle.
Jump to the top of the big line. Big line slides down.

Extra
Snip pieces of yarn. Make **Y** with yarn.
Glue yarn to a **Y** card.

Fun focus
Find everything that's yellow in the room. See who's wearing yellow.

Z

LITTLE LINE	+ BIG LINE	+ LITTLE LINE

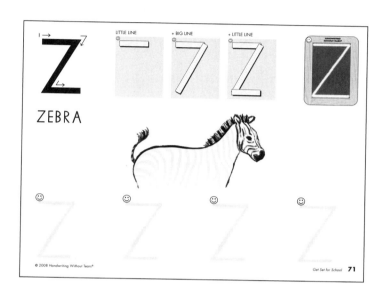

Ask about Z
Do you know: **Z** words? **Z** names? **Z** sounds?
Have you seen a zebra?

Begin to look and learn
This is the **Z** page. Let's find the **Z**s. (Point)
Look. There's a zebra. (Point)
Zebra starts with **Z**.
Talk about: what zebras eat, black stripes, four legs, tail, where they live.

Color and draw
Color the zebra stripes black.

Demonstrate tracing Z
Let's trace **Z**. Put the crayon on the ☺.
Little line across the top. Big line slides down.
Little line across.

Extra
Bring in pictures of zebras.

Fun focus
Sing a zoo animals version of the *Animal Legs* song, Track 13, and include a zebra.
Make 2 big curves into a huge zero and say zero.

Activity Page – ALPHABET REVIEW

So far, children have been tracing in developmental order. Now they're ready to learn letters in alphabetical order, as taught in these two pages. It's best to do these pages over three days or more, taking at least a day for letters at the beginning, middle, and end of the alphabet.

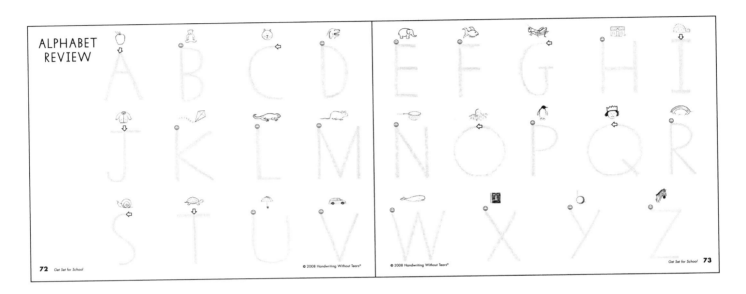

Ask about letters
Where is **A**? Is it in the beginning? Is it the first letter in the alphabet? What letter comes after **A**?
Can you find **M**? Is that the end of the alphabet?
No! **M** is in the middle of the alphabet.
Where is **Z**? Is it at the end of the alphabet? What letter comes after **Z**? None. **Z** is the last letter!

Begin to look and learn
Let's find letter **L**. What picture is above letter **L**?
Let's find letter **R**. What picture is above letter **R**?
What letter comes after **R**? What letter comes before **R**?

Color and trace
Trace the letters after the teacher's demonstration.
Day 1 - A B C D E F G H I   For fun, use blue to trace **B** and green for **G**. Use black for other letters.
Day 2 - J K L M N O P Q R   For fun, use purple or pink for **P**, red for **R**, and black for the other letters.
Day 3 - S T U V W X Y Z   For fun, use yellow to trace **Y** and color the yo-yo.

Demonstrate the letters
Let's trace the letters. Watch me write each letter, then you trace.

Extra
If you purchased a copy of this workbook for each student, you may copy these pages for extra practice for those students. Encourage correct letter formation by finger tracing before children write, or by demonstrating on your own copy of the page.

Activity Page – CAPITAL and Lowercase Letters

Here is the alphabet from the Pre-K Wall Cards. It's a page for learning to recognize lowercase letters and associating letters with pictures and beginning sounds. The pictures are too small for easy coloring, but children may like to trace or color a few of the square boxes.

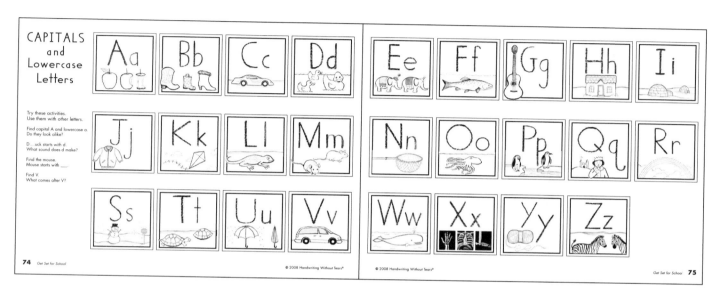

Ask about letters, sounds, and pictures
Find capital **A** and lowercase **a**. Do they look alike?
D…duck starts with **d**. What sound does **d** make?
Find the mouse. Mouse starts with ___.
Find the **V**. What comes after **V**?

Begin to look and learn
Letters have places in the alphabet. What letters are at the beginning? The end? The middle?
Find the first letter in your name. Find the first letter in your friend's name. Which comes first in the alphabet?

Count and color
Count how many things are on each letter card.

Demonstrate naming lowercase letters
Show how to hide the capital with your finger leaving just the lowercase.
Say, "I can't see the capital. Which letter is the lowercase letter?"
Show children how to do this with each other.

Extra
Challenge children to point to randomly named letters.
Challenge children to find the letter that comes after _____.
Challenge children to find the letter that comes before _____.

Children learn to recognize capital letters first, and then the lowercase letters that look like the capitals. It's tricky to learn the lowercase letters that don't look like capitals. This page will help.

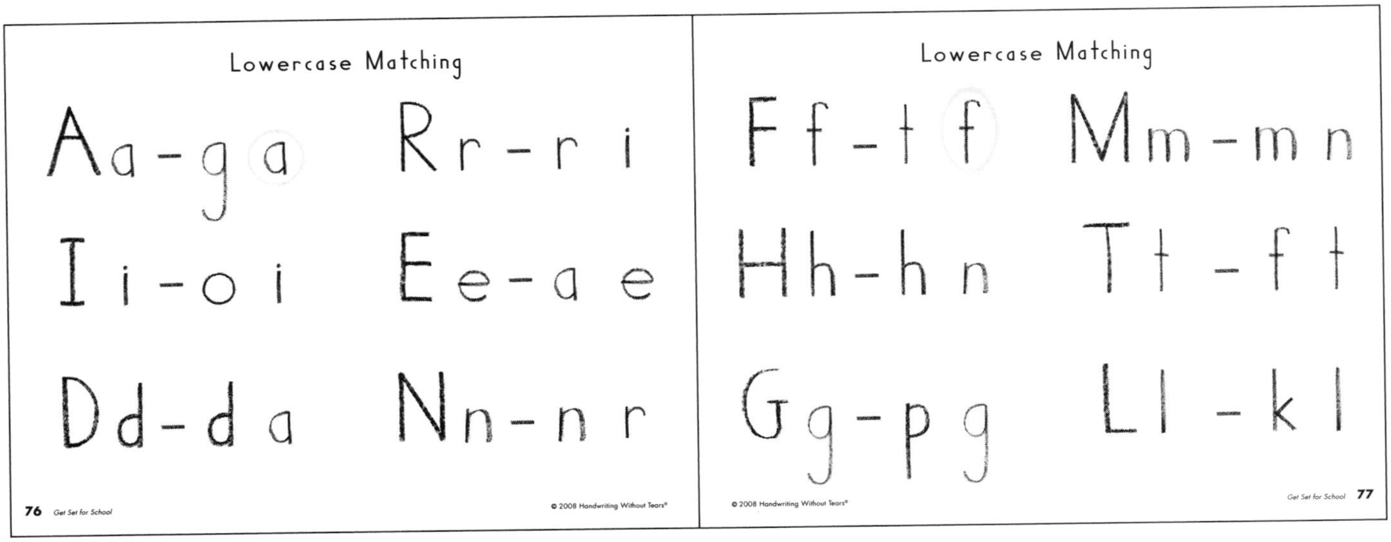

Lowercase Matching

A a - g a

I i - o i

D d - d a

R r - r i

E e - a e

N n - n r

Lowercase Matching

F f - t f

H h - h n

G g - p g

M m - m n

T t - f t

L l - k l

Ask about letters
Where is capital **A**?
What's beside capital **A**? Lowercase **a**.
Do capital **A** and lowercase **a** look alike?
What's beside lowercase **a**?
It's lowercase **g** and **a**.
Why is lowercase **a** circled? Because it matches.

Begin to look and learn
Let's find capital **R**.
What's beside capital **R**? Lowercase **r**.
Capital **R** and lowercase **r** do not look alike.
What's beside lowercase **r**? Lowercase **r** and **i**.
Which one matches?

Circle the matching lowercase letter
Make the circle start with a Magic c stroke.

Demonstrate matching and circling
Watch me write **R r - r i**.
Watch me circle the matching **r**.
I start the circle with a Magic c.

Extra
Find the letters that don't look like their capitals on the alphabet display on pages 74 and 75 of the workbook.

Activity Page – Five Fingers Play

From the time children first hold up their fingers to show how old they are, numbers are an important part of life. The program teaches numbers naturally through body awareness. The *Get Set For School Sing Along* CD songs: *Mat Man; Count On Me; Five Fingers Play; Bird Legs; Animal Legs; The Ant, the Bug, and the Bee;* and *Toe Song* give a physical understanding of numbers.

It's fun to learn numbers with songs about animals. Children sing, but they also move, touch, handle, and look as part of the song activities. For example: Children sing the *Animal Legs* song, Track 13, pick up a toy animal and count the legs: "2 legs in the front, 2 legs in the back, the horse has 4 legs!" This guide also has suggestions for using objects to teach numbers.

Children learn 1 2 3 4 5 by placing Wood Pieces on the mat and by using the HWT Slate Chalkboard. Children learn 6 7 8 9 on the Slate. See Wet–Dry–Try on page 112.
In the workbook, children point, count, color, and crayon trace numbers 1 2 3 4 5 6 7 8 9 10.

Help your children learn to:
1. **Count out loud**—Say the numbers 1 through 10 in order.
2. **Count with meaning**—Children learn the value of numbers 1 through 10. They count on themselves, animals and objects. They learn to touch and count.
3. **Build, recognize and trace Numbers**—Children become familiar with numbers using Wood Pieces, the Wet–Dry–Try Slate activity, and workbook lessons.

Teaching *Five Fingers Play*

FIVE FINGERS PLAY

One finger points

Two fingers walk

Three fingers stand up and talk, talk, talk

Four fingers count 1, 2, 3, 4

Oh look, I've got one more! Five fingers 1, 2, 3, 4, 5

Five fingers up

Five fingers down

Five fingers go round and round

Five fingers here

Five fingers there

Ten fingers to wash my hair

78 *Get Set for School*

© 2008 Handwriting Without Tears®

This finger play is also found on the *Get Set for School Sing Along* CD, Track 10. The activity uses movement and words to teach both body awareness and number skills.

NUMBERS
Teaching Wet–Dry–Try

The Wet–Dry–Try method is a sensory strategy for helping children learn numbers without reversals. This fun teaching method works for all learning styles: visual, auditory, tactile, and kinesthetic.

Gather Materials

Slate (1 per child)
Little Chalk Bits
Little Sponge Cubes
Paper Towels
Bowl of water

Teacher's Part

Demonstrate correct number formation.

Student's Part

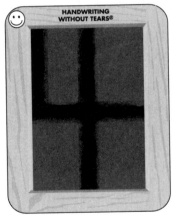

WET

- Wet Little Sponge Cube.
- Squeeze it out.
- Trace the letter with the sponge.
- Wet your finger and trace again.

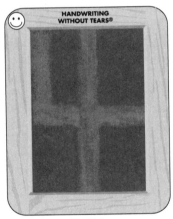

DRY

- Crumple a little paper towel.
- Dry the letter a few times.
- Gently blow for final drying.

TRY

- Take a Little Chalk Bit.
- Use it to write the letter.

Tips for Teachers

- Use Little Sponge Cubes and Little Chalk Bits—smaller pieces develop pencil grip.
- Squeeze the sponge well or the number will be too wet.
- This works best one–on–one or in centers with five or fewer students.
- To use this activity with the whole class, you must pre–mark each student's slate with the number (so they have a correct model to wet), and then demonstrate once for everyone.

Number Activity – *Number Song*

Sing and Write Numbers in the Air

The *Number Song* appeals to preschool children. It can be found on *The Rock Rap Tap and Learn* CD, Track 20. Play it in the background over several days until you and the children are familiar with the tune and the words. Then sing it with the CD, encouraging children to sing with you. When they can follow the words, use it as a song for *Air Writing* (see page 58).

Do not play the CD, just sing as you model big numbers in the air. At first, just do one and two. Another day, you can try numbers up to three. Children will take a little while to be able to sing and follow the motions, but they'll learn and enjoy this activity. Children will enjoy the challenge of adding more numbers as one, two, three become more secure.

Number Song

Numbers are great
And numbers are fun
Let's all start with the number **1**
Start at the top
Make a big line
Your number **1**, it looks just fine
For number **2**, now what do we do?
Make a big curve and a little line too
Your **2** looks great
But don't be late
3 is next and we just can't wait

Chorus
Numbers, numbers
Not toys or cars or cucumbers
Hey did you ever wonder
How we could count without numbers?

To make number **3** oh all we need
Are two little curves just wait and see
A little curve once and a little curve twice
The **3** is done and it looks so nice
Here comes **4** it rhymes with door
Make two little lines and a big line more
The **4** is through now what should we do?
5 comes next that's just a clue

Chorus

With number **5** now what do we do?
Drop a little line and a little curve too
Then jump back up to the top
Add a little line and then you stop

Start number **6** at the top like this
Drop a line down and do the curvy trick
Write it again just for fun
6 is a slippery slidey one

Chorus

7 is easy, so easy to do
A little line across and slide down too
We're counting higher all the time
Just remember **7** has two lines
Number **8** is so much fun
Start with **s** then up to the sun
Write it big and write it small
That wasn't very hard at all

Chorus

We're counting higher to number **9**
Write a little curve and one big line
Write it once, write it twice
99 is mighty nice

Can you write a number **10**?
You get to use the **1** again
Draw a **0** next to one
Now your **10** is really done
We wrote the numbers **1** to **10**
What comes next?
Write them again

Chorus

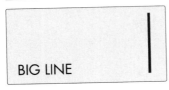

BIG LINE

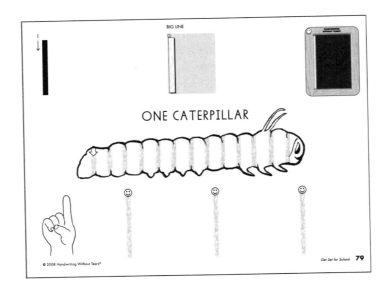

1 Caterpillar

Directions

Aim crayon at ☺. Big line down.
- Finger trace the number one at the top of the page.
- Teach one with Wood Pieces and on the Slate.
- Count one caterpillar. Color the caterpillar.
- Make one with your finger.
- Trace each number one with a crayon.

1 with Bodies—Count on me! Animals too!
- Hold up one finger to show **1**.
- Use the *Get Set for School Sing Along* CD.
    Play *Five Fingers Play*, Track 10. Point with one finger.
- Count **1** on people. Count down the center.
    1 head, 1 forehead, 1 nose, 1 mouth, 1 chin, 1 neck, 1 chest, 1 belly button.

1 with Objects—Count and compare
- Touch and count things one by one in an organized way. Line up objects and count from left to right.
- Turn pages one by one.
- 1 on 1   At snack or mealtime, help children put 1 napkin on each mat, etc.
- 1 to 1   Talk about the relationship of baby/crib, horse/saddle, head/hat, hot dog/ bun.
- Give just one when children ask for something. Then ask, "Do you want another one?"

Number 1—See and say
- See **1** and say, "one."
- Look for numbers. Find **1**.
- Say "first" and "first one." Talk about firsts—grade, day of school, birthday, snow of winter, star in the sky.
- Use "first" in a sequence. For example: First we put on our coats and then we go outside.
- Say who or what is first in a line. For example: A locomotive is the first car in the train.

Teach

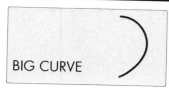
BIG CURVE

LITTLE LINE

2 Legs

Ask about bird legs
How many legs does the duck have?
Chick? Rooster? Ostrich? Crane? Flamingo?

Begin to look and learn
These birds are different.
Look at their necks, heads, beaks, bodies.

Color the birds
Use a book to show pictures of the birds in color.
Find the flamingo on the PINK page.

Demonstrate tracing legs down
Watch me make bird legs.
(Do left leg first, as if starting letter **H**.)

Extra
Use the *Get Set for School Sing Along* CD.
Play *Bird Legs*, Track 12.

Stamp a simple bird shape along the bottom of a page
leaving room for children to draw 2 legs on each.

2 Chicks

Directions: Aim crayon at ☺. Big curve. Little line.
- Finger trace the two at the top of the page.
- Teach two with Wood Pieces and on the Slate.
- Count two chicks. Two legs. Color the chicks.
- Hold up two fingers.
- Trace each number two with a crayon.

2 with Bodies—Count on me! Birds too!
- Hold up two fingers to show **2**.
- Count 2 on our bodies with two fingers. Point to:
  2 eyebrows, eyes, ears, cheeks, arms, etc.
- Use the *Get Set for School Sing Along* CD.
  Play *Bird Legs*, Track 12. Add verses for 2 wings
  and 2 eyes.

2 with Objects—Count and compare
- Count **2** on clothing:
  2 shoes, socks, mittens, sleeves, pant legs.
- Sort and match pairs by color and size.
- Share 2: 1 for me and 1 for you.
  Cut something in half to share.
- Count 2 wheels on bicycles.
- Put 2 candles on a cake and count.

Numbers 2—See and say
- See **2** and say, "two." Find **2**.
- Find numbers in Nursery Rhymes: "One, two,
  button my shoe," etc.

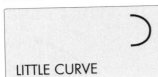

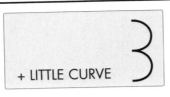

LITTLE CURVE   + LITTLE CURVE

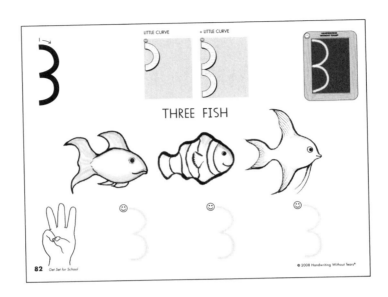

3 Fish

Directions: Aim crayon at ☺. Little curve. Little curve.

- Finger trace the three at the top of the page.
- Teach three with Wood Pieces and on the Slate.
- Count three fish. Color the three fish.
- Hold up three fingers.
- Trace each number three with a crayon.

3 with Bodies—Count on me!
- Hold up three fingers to show **3**.
- Use the *Get Set for School Sing Along* CD.
  Play *Five Fingers Play*, Track 10.
      Do the motions for 3 fingers stand up and talk,
      talk, talk."

3 with Objects—Count and compare
- Count 3 wheels on a tricycle.
- Build a bridge with 2 cubes on bottom and 1 on top.
- Build a triangle with 3 big lines. Count 3 sides and 3 angles.
- Sort by category. Mix up 3 cars and 3 planes for child to divide into groups.
- Get ready with counting: 1...2...3...go!

Number 3—See and say
- See **3** and say, "three."
- Look for numbers. Find **3**.
- Say "third." Do the children know a third grader?
- Baseball? Show children first, second, and third base. Run to third!
- Find 3 in Nursery Rhymes :
  Old King Cole, Three Blind Mice, Rub a dub, dub, three men in a tub.

© 2008 Handwriting Without Tears

| LITTLE LINE | + LITTLE LINE | + BIG LINE |

FOUR ANIMALS

© 2008 Handwriting Without Tears®   *Get Set for School* **83**

4 Animals

Directions: Aim crayon at ☺. Little line down. Little line across. Jump to the top. Big line down.
- Finger trace the four at the top of the page.
- Teach four with Wood Pieces and on the Slate.
- Count four animals. Trace four legs.
- Hold up four fingers.
- Trace each number four with a crayon.

4 with Bodies—Count on me! Animals too!
- Hold up four fingers to show **4**. How old are you?
- Creep on all fours.
- Use the *Get Set for School Sing Along* CD.
  Play *Five Fingers Play*, Track 10.
  Play *Animal Legs*, Track 13.
    Personalize this song. Put four legged animals into a basket.
    Sing as each child takes a turn with an animal from the basket.

4 with Objects—Count and compare
- Count 4 legs on chairs, 4 legs on tables and 4 wheels on cars!
- Build a square with 4 big lines.
- Count 4 on a square napkin, 4 sides/4 corners. Open up the napkin and see 4 more squares.
- Count 4 birthday candles. How old are you?

Number 4—See and say
- See **4** and say, "four."
- Look for numbers. Find **4**.
  Say "fourth." Teach American about the Fourth of July.
- Teach four year old children to say, "I am 4 years old."
- Find 4 in Nursery Rhymes: "4 and 20 blackbirds baked in a pie." "One, two, buckle my shoe...."

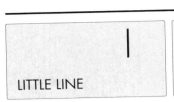

LITTLE LINE	+ LITTLE CURVE	+ LITTLE LINE

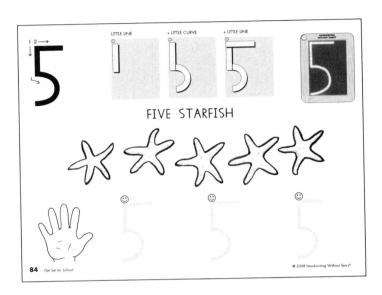

5 Starfish

Directions: Aim crayon at ☺. Little line down. Little curve. Jump to the ☺. Little line across.
- Finger trace the five at the top of the page.
- Teach five with Wood Pieces and on the Slate.
- Count five starfish. Count 5 points on the starfish. Color five starfish.
- Hold up five fingers.
- Trace each number five with a crayon.

5 with Bodies—Count on me! Animals too!
- Hold up your hand to show 5 fingers.
- Give 5. Teach children how to give a high 5.
- Count 5 arms on the starfish.
- Count 5 toes on one foot. Now count 5 toes on the other foot!
- Use the *Get Set for School Sing Along* CD. Play *Five Fingers Play*, Track 10.
  Play *Toes Song*, Track 11.

5 with Objects—Count and compare
- Touch and count 5 objects.
- Count the points on a star.
- Count 5 birthday candles.

Number 5—See and say
- See **5** and say, "five".
- Look for numbers. Find **5** on a calendar.
- Teach 5 year olds to say, "I am 5 years old."
- Say "fifth."
- Play finger games with 5: "This is the beehive, Where are the bees?"
- Say the 5 days of the school week: Monday, Tuesday, Wednesday, Thursday, and Friday.

| LINE DOWN CURVE | CURL AROUND |

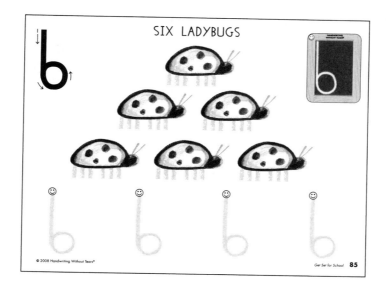

SIX LADYBUGS

© 2008 Handwriting Without Tears®   *Get Set for School* **85**

6 Ladybugs

Directions: Aim crayon at ☺. Go down. Curl around.
- Finger trace the six at the top of the page.
- Teach six on the Slate.
- Count six ladybugs. Count six legs on each lady bug. Color six ladybugs.
- Trace each number six with a crayon.

6 with Bodies—Count on me! Insects too!
- Hold up one hand for 5. Add one finger on the other hand for **6**.
- Use the *Get Set for School Sing Along* CD.
  Play *The Ant, the Bug and the Bee,* Track 14
      Show children the hand motions: Hold up 3 fingers on each hand to show **6** for "6 little legs." Walk them up and down in the air. Tuck fingers in armpits when "they fly around."

6 with Objects—Count and compare
- Touch and count 6 objects.
- Build a pyramid with 6 cubes, 3 on bottom, 2 in the middle, 1 on top.
- Put 6 eggs in an egg carton. Compare 6 eggs and 6 empty places.

6 Numbers—To see and say
- See **6** and say, "six."
- Say "sixth."
- Look for numbers. Find **6** on a computer or calculator.
- Teach children to say dozen for 12 and half dozen for 6.
  Many children know these words from bagels or donuts.

LITTLE LINE ACROSS	—	BIG LINE SLIDE DOWN	7

7 Turtles

Directions: Aim crayon at ☺. Little line across. Big line slides down.
- Finger trace the seven at the top of the page.
- Count seven turtles. Color seven turtles.
- Trace seven on the Slate.
- Trace each number seven with a crayon.

7 with Objects—Count and compare
- Touch and count 7 objects.
- Build a tower with 7 cubes.

7 Numbers—To see and say
- See **7** and say, "seven."
- Look for numbers. Find **7** on a calendar or in a book.
- Look and count to 7 on a computer or calculator.
- Say, "seven days in the week."
- Fairy tale: *Snow White and the Seven Dwarfs.*

The **S** part of the **8** is made with a wider crayon stroke so children notice the **S**. If they make the **S** correctly, then the rest is easy.

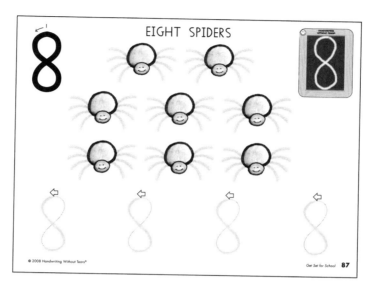

8 Spiders

Directions: Aim the crayon at the arrow. Begin with letter **S**. Back up to the top.
- Finger trace the eight at the top of the page.
- Count eight spiders. Count eight spider legs. Color eight spiders.
- Trace eight on the slate.
- Trace each number eight with a crayon.

8 with Bodies—Count on me! Spider and octopus too!
- Count legs on a spider.
- Use the *Get Set for School Sing Along* CD.
  Play *Spiders Love to Party*, Track 15
      Show the hand motions. Hold up 4 fingers on each hand to show 8 legs for dancing.
      Dance around with 8 legs dancing in the air.
- Count legs on an octopus.

8 with Objects—Count and compare
- Touch and count 8 objects.
- Build a tower with 8 cubes.
- Count wheels on 2 cars.
- Craft—Make spiders by having children trace hands on folded black paper with white chalk.
  Teacher cuts this out and cuts off the thumb. When opened, there's a spider.

Number 8—See and say
- See **8** and say, "eight."
- Count by twos: 2, 4, 6, 8.
- Look for numbers. Find **8**.
- Find **8** on a clock. Is bedtime 8 o'clock?
  When does school start?

Here is a fun review of counting using animal legs.

2 - 4 - 6 - 8 Legs

Ask about legs
Do these animals have the same number of legs?
Which animals have four legs?
Which animal has more legs? An octopus or a bear?

Begin to look and learn
Look at **2**. The goose and the chick have two legs.
Look at **4**. The polar bear and buffalo have four legs.
Look at **6**. The ant and the ladybug have six legs.
Look at **8**. The octopus and the spider have eight legs.

Color the animals
Show color pictures of a buffalo, chick, ladybug...

Demonstrate tracing legs down
(Do just the legs, as if writing tally marks from left to right.)
Watch me make **2** legs. Down **1**... **2**... Your turn.
Watch me make **4** legs. Down **1** ... **2**... **3**... **4**.
Watch me make **6** little legs. Down **1** ... **2**... **3**... **4**...**5**...**6**.
Watch me make **8** legs. **1** ... **2**... **3**... **4**... on this side. **1** ...**2**... **3**... **4**... on this side to make **8**.

Extra
- Use the *Get Set for School Sing Along* CD.
  Play a track for any number, **2** - **4** - **6** - **8**.
  2 - *Bird legs*, Track 12   **4** - *Animal Legs*, Track 13
  6 - *The Ant, the Bug, and the Bee*, Track 14   **8** - *Spider Love to Party*, Track 15

| LITTLE CURVE | UP INTO THE CORNER | BIG LINE DOWN |

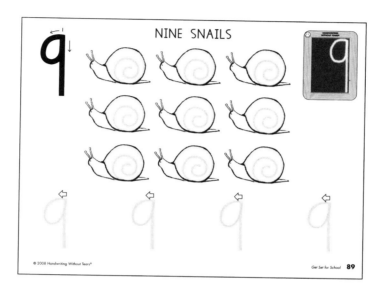

9 Snails

Directions: Aim crayon at arrow. Little curve around and up. Big line down.
- Finger trace the nine at the top of the page.
- Count nine snails. Color nine snails.
- Trace nine on the Slate.
- Trace each number nine with a crayon.

9 with Hands and Objects—Count and compare
- Touch and count **9** objects.
- Build a tower with **9** cubes.
- Let's do **9** with our hands.
  Show me **9** like this: 5 fingers + 4 fingers.
- Let's do **9** with three people
  Each person hold up **3** hands.
  Let's count: **1 2 3   4 5 6   7 8 9**.

Number 9—See and say
- See **9** and say, "nine."
- Look for numbers. Find **9**.
- Look and count to 9 on a computer or calculator.

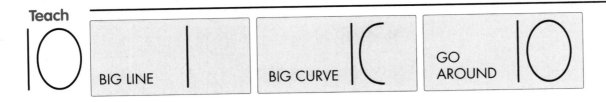

| BIG LINE | | BIG CURVE | | GO AROUND | |

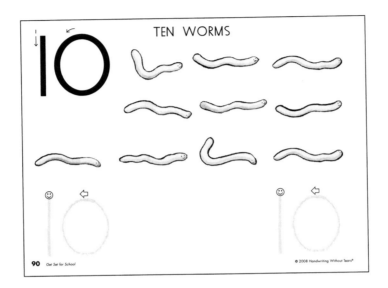

TEN WORMS

90   *Get Set for School*   © 2008 Handwriting Without Tears®

10 Worms

Directions: Aim crayon at arrow. Big line. Big Curve. Go Around.
- Finger trace the ten at the top of the page.
- Count ten worms. Color ten worms.
- Trace each number ten with a crayon.

10 with Bodies—Count on me! Fingers and Toes!
- Hold up one hand for 5 and another hand for 5. That's 10 fingers!
- Use the *Five Fingers Play* chant on the *Get Set for School Sing Along* CD, Track 10.
- Count toes on one foot. Now count the toes on the other foot!
- Sing the *Toe Song* on the *Get Set for School Sing Along* CD, Track 11.

10 with Objects—To count and compare
- Touch and count 10 objects.
- Touch and count 10 pennies.
  Put 10 pennies in a bank.
- Look at a dime. It is equal to 10 pennies.

10 Numbers—To see and say
- See **10** and say, "ten."
- Look for numbers. Find **10**.
- Look and count to 10 on a computer or calculator.
- Say "tenth."
- Count backward from 10.

Number Review

Review numbers with children by having them trace and count from 1-10.

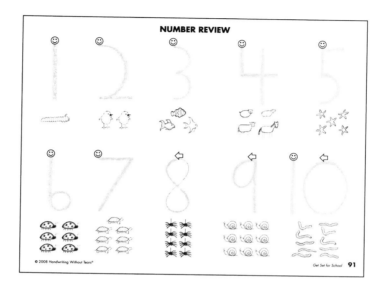

Ask about numbers
Where is **6**?
What number comes after **4**?
Can you find number **9**?

Begin to look and learn
Let's look at the ladybugs. How many are there ?
      Let's make six with our hands.
      Show me 6 like this: 5 fingers + 1 finger.
      Show me 6 like this: 3 fingers + 3 fingers.
Let's look at the spiders. How many are there?
      Let's make eight with our hands.
      Show me 8 like this: 5 fingers + 3 fingers.
      Show me 8 like this: 4 fingers + 4 fingers.

Color and trace
Trace the numbers after the teacher's demonstration.

Demonstrate the numbers
Let's trace the numbers. Watch me write each number, then you trace.

Extra
If you have purchased a copy of this workbook for each student, you may copy this page for extra practice. Encourage correct number formation by demonstrating, saying the words, or by having children show you finger tracing before writing.

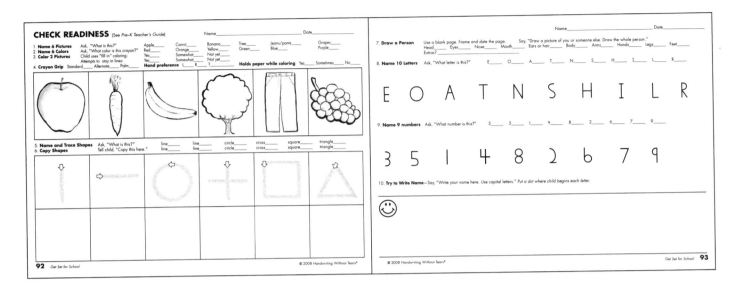

General Directions:

Check each correct item. Write in other answers and observations.

1. Name 6 Pictures

Typically, this is easy for English speaking children. When asking a non-verbal child to point, name the pictures in random order.

2. Name 6 Colors

Use crayons with true colors. Ask a child to say the colors as you point.

3. Color 2 Pictures

Let the child choose the pictures to color. Notice how a child picks up and uses crayons. Record this on the next item.

4. Crayon Grip
Hand Preference
Holds Paper

See pages 64-65 for information about these skills.
Note which hand is used. Mark a "?" if a child changes hands when coloring.

5. Name and Trace Shapes

Children may use other words, for example: one for line, or ball for circle. Simply write a child's words on the page. Tell the child to start on the arrow and trace the shapes.

6. Copy Shapes

As soon as a child finishes tracing each shape, make a dot to show the starting place. This will make you aware of a child's starting tendency.

7. Draw a Person

Name, date, and save these. Check the 10 parts and note any extras.

8. Name 10 Letters

Naming letters out of order shows true recognition. Write in any wrong answers. When asking a non-verbal child to point, say the letters in random order.

9. Name 9 Numbers

Write in any wrong answers. When asking a non-verbal child to point, say the numbers in random order.

10. Try to Write Name

Tell children to start at the ☺. As soon as a child writes a letter, make a dot to show the starting place.

EXTRAS
Educating Others

Because handwriting often takes a back seat in today's elementary schools, it's wonderful for someone knowledgeable in handwriting, specifically the Handwriting Without Tears® method, to step forward and share that knowledge with others. Whether you are educating parents at a back-to-school night or presenting in front of a language arts committee, the information you share will improve the likelihood that others will recognize the importance of teaching handwriting.

Parents
Educate parents about the Get Set For School™ program. This letter will educate parents and give them access to our website. **Go to www.hwtears.com/click** for a copy of this letter. Print it, sign it, and send it home.

Colleagues
Share your HWT knowledge with your friends and co-workers. If you have attended or plan to attend our workshops, tell friends about it. Better yet—invite them to come along. Often, all it takes is one teacher from a school getting excited about handwriting to inspire an entire school to learn more.

Administrators and Committees
Principals can be your biggest advocates. Share the information you have learned with principals and other administrators. Discuss the benefits of handwriting consistency and how HWT can help. Many HWT advocates have successfully written proposals, initiated handwriting pilot studies, presented to language arts committees, and seen large districts adopt HWT district-wide. Email or call us for help—janolsen@hwtears.com or 301-263-2700. We will send you a CD loaded with everything you need to help others understand that handwriting should be an easy victory for children and how using the Handwriting Without Tears® program enables that success.

Helpful Handouts

Giving parents letter/number charts and other helpful information at the start of school helps them understand how to form letters and gives them ideas of how to help their child at home. You can find parent articles to print and distribute on the website. Articles, similar to the one below, can be helpful to you as well. If parents are able to practice just 5 minutes a day with their child, the results can be amazing. We provided you with this first article, "Help Me Hold the Crayon," on the next page because we think learning to hold a crayon is so critical that we wanted to make sure you had it right away. Copy it and send it home the first week of school.

Also try:

1. Singing with parents *Where Do You Start Your Letters at the Top?* during parent night at your school.
2. Providing handouts during parent/teacher conferences.
3. Sending them home with students that are new to your room.
4. Sharing them with colleagues.

Use Mat Man™ to Teach Body Awareness

Show children how to build Mat Man using the Mat, Capital Letter Wood Pieces and a few accessories.

Mat Man
Tune: The Bear Went Over the Mountain

Mat Man has	1 head,	1 head,	1 head,	Mat Man has	1 head,	So that he can*	think
Mat Man has	2 eyes,	2 eyes,	2 eyes,	*(repeat)*	2 eyes,	*(repeat)*	see
Mat Man has	1 nose,	1 nose,	1 nose,		1 nose,		smell
Mat Man has	1 mouth,	1 mouth,	1 mouth,		1 mouth,		eat
Mat Man has	2 ears,	2 ears,	2 ears,		2 ears,		hear
Mat Man has	1 body,	1 body,	1 body,		1 body,	To hold what is inside	heart, lungs, stomach
Mat Man has	2 arms,	2 arms,	2 arms,		2 arms,	So that he can*	reach
Mat Man has	2 hands,	2 hands,	2 hands,		2 hands,	*(repeat)*	clap
Mat Man has	2 legs,	2 legs,	2 legs,		2 legs,		stand
Mat Man has	2 feet,	2 feet,	2 feet,		2 feet,		walk

* Wait for your children to respond. Add extra verses when you add new accessories. Your children may call out other body functions (feet= run, kick, dance). Encourage this while keeping the song/activity moving along.

Fine Motor and Letter Practice for Home

Hand skills are crucial to successful handwriting. Small movements of the hand are referred to as fine motor skills. If you feel your child is in need of extra activities to strengthen his hands or fine motor skills look at here are a few suggestions:

- Do finger–plays. Find them in a book at the library.
- Cut pictures out of newspapers or magazines. You can take a large black marker and draw a line around the picture to give a guideline.
- Have your child put together small beads, Lego's, Tinker Toys, Lincoln Logs, etc.
- Knead Play dough or clay. Build objects with them.
- Hide small objects in the Play dough and have your child find them.
- Play pegboard games.
- Gather small objects from around the house (small buttons, beads, etc.) place them in a container and have your child pick them up off the table with a pair of tweezers and place them back in the container.
- Play with any toys that require moving or placing little pieces.
- Let your children squirt water bottle outdoors on the sidewalk. Colored water looks great on the snow.
- Squeeze a kitchen baster to move a cotton balls with air. Have a race on the table..
- Finger paint with Jell-O or Cocoa on a paper plate.
- Use small marshmallows and toothpicks to form letters.
- String, popcorn, buttons, beads to make necklaces.
- Using a hole-punch let your child create a design on a piece of paper.
- Have your children clip clothespins to a container.
- Have children lace cards.

You can do several fun activities at home to encourage letter practice. A few are listed below:

- While your children is in the bathtub have them draw letters on the wall of the tub in shaving cream or soap paint.
- Trace a letter on your child's back and have them guess and write the letter on a piece of paper. Take turns and have them trace a letter on your back.
- Finger paint letters.
- Write letters on the sidewalk with chalk.
- Trace letters in the snow or sand.
- Forms letters out of play dough or clay.
- Make cookie letters. Having your child form the letters by rolling the dough and putting the pieces together.
- Form letters out of French Fries.
- Make letters with pipe cleaners.
- Draw letters with your finger on the carpet.
- Decorate a letter collage using glitter, puffy paint, and markers.
- Use different types of pencils for writing practice (gel pens, colored pencils, scented markers, crayons, etc.)
- Have your children write your shopping lists.
- Use a flashlight and make letters on the wall. You or your child has to guess the letter that was made. You can also cut out letter templates to place in front of the flashlight.
- Put letters on a die and have your child roll the dice and they have to write a word that starts with the letter.
- Fish for words. Place cut out fish in a shoebox. Write words or letters on the fish. Attach paper clips to the fish and adapt a small pole with a magnet. Whichever fish the child gets, they have to come up with a word or sentence using what is on the fish.
- Have children write with icing tubes.

Help Me Hold the Crayon

There are easy ways to help your child. Even if you're not a teacher, and don't hold the pencil correctly yourself, you can still be a very good influence on your child. Here's how:

1. Choose the correct writing tools.
2. Show your child how to hold them.
3. Be a good example.

How do I choose the correct writing tools?

- As soon as your child is past age 3 or the putting-things-in-mouth swallowing stage, give him or her little broken pieces of chalk or crayon and lots of big sheets of paper for loose scribbling/drawing.
- Little pieces of finger food also encourage finger skills.

Why little pieces?

Little pieces develop fingertip control and strength. They encourage the precise pinch that's used for crayons and pencils. Notice how well your child uses his/her fingers with little pieces. There's research to show that starting with small pieces encourages the correct grasp.

What about regular crayons and pencils?

They're fine, but you must show your child how to hold and use them. Save the pencils for later. Pencils are sharp pointed sticks and really aren't appropriate for beginners. Fat pencils and crayons are too heavy for little hands.

When should I start?

Right now. You can start showing your child how to use crayons as soon as your child wants to color.

How do I show my child?

1. Teach your child to name the first 3 fingers – the thumb, the pointer, and the tall man.
2. Move them – Give a thumbs up and wiggle the thumb. Have your child point with the pointer finger and then put the tall man beside the pointer finger.
3. Make a big open O pinch – this positions the thumb and pointer correctly.

What is the correct grip?

Here's a picture. Notice that there is a choice. Some children like to pinch with the thumb and pointer. That's the tripod (3-pinch with thumb and pointer, pencil rests on tall man). Others like the quadropod (4–pinch with thumb and pointer/tall man together, pencil rests on ring finger).

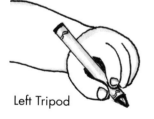
Left Tripod

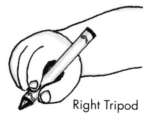
Right Tripod

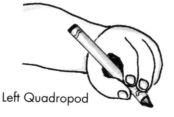
Left Quadropod

Right Quadropod

What else can I do?

1. Pick up and Drop it! This is a fun way to practice placing the fingers correctly. Help your child pick up the pencil and get all the fingers placed. Then drop it! See if your child can put all the fingers back in the right place again. Repeat two or three times.
2. Aim and Scribble. Make tiny stars or spots on paper. Teach your child how to aim the crayon and land on a star to make it shine. Help the crayon hand rest on the paper, with the elbow down and the hand touching the paper. Help the helper hand hold the paper. Now just wiggle the fingers to scribble.
3. Show your child how to hold and move the crayon to make different strokes, back and forth, up and down, round and round.

Teaching Guidelines

The HWT curriculum is highly adaptable and can be used in a number of ways. If you are looking for a completely structured approach, we have created these guidelines to help you along.

Week	Monday	Tuesday	Wednesday	Thursday	Friday
1	**Wood Pieces Activity** TGPK pg. 35-36	***Get Set For School Sing Along* CD** *Hello Song* Track 7	***Get Set For School Sing Along* CD** *Alphabet Song* Track 2	**Wood Pieces Activity** TGPK pg. 37	***Get Set For School Sing Along* CD** *Hello Song* Track 7
2	***Get Set For School Sing Along* CD** *Alphabet Song* Track 2	**Wood Pieces Activity** TGPK pg. 38	***Get Set For School Sing Along* CD** *10 Little Fingers* Track 16	**Wood Pieces Activity** TGPK pg. 39	**Wood Pieces Activity** TGPK pg. 40
3	**Wood Pieces Activity** TGPK pg. 41	***Get Set For School Sing Along* CD** *Where Do You Start Your Letters?* Track 1	**Mat Man Activity** TGPK pg. 46-50	***Get Set For School Sing Along* CD** *Mat Man* Track 8	**Review Wood Pieces Activities** TGPK pg. 35-41
4	**Aim & Scribble** TGPK pg. 70 GSS pg. 5	**Wood Pieces & Capital Letter Cards**	**Aim & Scribble** TGPK pg. 70 GSS pg. 6-7	***Get Set For School Sing Along* CD** *Where Do You Start Your Letters?* *Repeat Tuesday Activity	**Activity Page** TGPK pg. 71 GSS pg. 8-9
5	**Wood Pieces & Capital Letter Cards**	**Coloring Pictures** Red & Green TGPK pg. 72 GSS pg. 10-11	***Get Set For School Sing Along* CD** *Where Do You Start Your Letters?* *Repeat Monday Activity	**Coloring Pictures** Yellow & Purple TGPK pg. 73 GSS pg. 12-13	**Review with Wood Pieces & Capital Letter Cards**
6	**Coloring Pictures** Blue & Orange TGPK pg. 74 GSS pg. 14-15	**Wood Pieces & Capital Letter Cards**	**Coloring Pictures** Pink & Brown TGPK pg. 75 GSS pg. 16-17	***Get Set For School Sing Along* CD** *Where Do You Start Your Letters?* *Repeat Tuesday Activity	**Coloring Pages** Gray & Black TGPK pg. 76 GSS pg. 18-19
7	**Mat Man Activity** TGPK pg. 77 GSS pg. 20-21	**Wood Pieces & Capital Letter Cards**	**Activity Page** TGPK pg. 78 GSS pg. 22-23	**Wood Pieces & Capital Letter Cards**	**Activity Page** Cross TGPK pg. 79 GSS pg. 24
8	**L** **Wood Pieces & Slate** TGPK pg. 79	**L** **Crayon Stroke** GSS pg. 25	**Activity Page** Square TGPK pg. 80 GSS pg. 26	**F** **Wood Pieces & Slate** TGPK pg. 80	**F** **Crayon Stroke** GSS pg. 27
9	**E Pre-Stroke** TGPK pg. 81 GSS pg. 28	**E** **Wood Pieces & Slate** TGPK pg. 81	**E** **Crayon Stroke** GSS pg. 29	**Activity Page** Rectangle TGPK pg. 82 GSS pg. 30	***Get Set For School Sing Along* CD** *Where Do You Start Your Letters?*
10	**Review with Wood Pieces & Slate** L F E	**H** **Wood Pieces & Slate** TGPK pg. 82	**H** **Crayon Stroke** GSS pg. 31	**T** **Wood Pieces & Slate** TGPK pg. 83	**T** **Crayon Stroke** GSS pg. 32
11	**I** **Wood Pieces & Slate** TGPK pg. 84	**I** **Crayon Stroke** GSS pg. 33	**Coloring Page** TGPK pg. 85 GSS pg. 34	**U** **Wood Pieces & Slate** TGPK pg. 85	**U** **Crayon Stroke** GSS pg. 35
12	**Review Capitals with Wood Pieces & Slates** H T I U	**Magic C Activity** *Get Set For School Sing Along* CD Track 6 TGPK pg. 86	**Pre-Stroke C** TGPK pg. 87 GSS pg. 36	**C** **Wood Pieces & Slate** TGPK pg. 87	**C** **Crayon Stroke** GSS pg. 37

Week	Monday	Tuesday	Wednesday	Thursday	Friday
13	**Pre-Stroke O** TGPK pg. 88 GSS pg. 38	**O** **Wood Pieces & Slate** TGPK pg. 88	**O** **Crayon Stroke** GSS pg. 39	**Activity Page** TGPK pg. 89 GSS pg. 40	**Q** **Wood Pieces & Slate** TGPK pg. 89
14	**Q** **Crayon Stroke** GSS pg. 41	**Pre-Stroke G** TGPK pg. 90 GSS pg. 42	**G** **Wood Pieces & Slate** TGPK pg. 90	**G** **Crayon Stroke** GSS pg. 43	**Number 1** TGPK pg. 114 GSS pg. 79
15	*Get Set For School* *Sing Along* **CD** *Alphabet Song* Track 2	**Review with Wood** **Pieces & Slates** C O Q G	**Pre-Stroke S** TGPK pg. 91 GSS pg. 44	**S** **Wood Pieces & Slate** TGPK pg. 91	**Number 2** TGPK pg. 115 GSS pg. 81
16	**S** **Crayon Stroke** GSS pg. 45	**Pre-Stroke J** TGPK pg. 92 GSS pg. 46	**J** **Wood Pieces & Slate** TGPK pg. 92	**J** **Crayon Stroke** GSS pg. 47	**Number 3** TGPK pg. 116 GSS pg. 82
17	**Pre-Stroke D** TGPK pg. 93 GSS pg. 48	**D** **Wood Pieces & Slate** TGPK pg. 93	**D** **Crayon Stroke** GSS pg. 49	*Get Set For School* *Sing Along* **CD** *Ten Little Fingers* Track 16	**Number 4** TGPK pg. 117 GSS pg. 83
18 Review	**Review with Wood** **Pieces & Slate** L F E	**Review with Wood** **Pieces & Slate** H T I U	**Review with Wood** **Pieces & Slate** C O Q G	**Review with Wood** **Pieces & Slate** S J D	**Number 5** TGPK pg. 118 GSS pg. 84
19	**P** **Wood Pieces & Slate** TGPK pg. 94	**P** **Crayon Stroke** GSS pg. 50	**B** **Wood Pieces & Slate** TGPK pg. 95	**B** **Crayon Stroke** GSS pg. 51	**Number 6** TGPK pg. 119 GSS pg. 85
20	**Pre-Stroke R** TGPK pg. 96 GSS pg. 52	**R** **Wood Pieces & Slate** TGPK pg. 96	**R** **Crayon Stroke** GSS pg. 53	**Review with Wood** **Pieces & Slate** P B R	**Number 7** TGPK pg.120 GSS pg. 86
21	**Pre-Stroke K** TGPK pg. 97 GSS pg. 54	**K** **Wood Pieces & Slate** TGPK pg. 97	**K** **Crayon Stroke** GSS pg. 55	**Pre-Stroke A** TGPK pg. 98 GSS pg. 56	**Number 8** TGPK pg. 121 GSS pg. 87
22	**A** **Wood Pieces & Slate** TGPK pg. 98	**A** **Crayon Stroke** GSS pg. 57	**Shape Page** TGPK pg. 99 GSS pg. 58	**Shape Page** TGPK pg. 99 GSS pg. 59	**Number 9** TGPK pg. 123 GSS pg. 89
23	**Pre-Stroke V** TGPK pg. 100 GSS pg. 60	**V** **Wood Pieces & Slate** TGPK pg. 100	**V** **Crayon Stroke** GSS pg. 61	**Review with Wood** **Pieces & Slate** K A V	**Number 10** TGPK pg. 124 GSS pg. 90
24	**Pre-Stroke M** TGPK pg. 101 GSS pg. 62	**M** **Wood Pieces & Slate** TGPK pg. 101	**M** **Crayon Stroke** GSS pg. 63	**Pre-Stroke N** TGPK pg. 102 GSS pg. 64	**Number Review** TGPK pg. 125 GSS pg. 91
25	**N** **Wood Pieces & Slate** TGPK pg. 102	**N** **Crayon Stroke** GSS pg. 65	**Activity Page** TGPK pg. 103 GSS pg. 66-67	**W** **Wood Pieces & Slate** TGPK pg. 104	**W** **Crayon Stroke** GSS pg. 68
26	**Review with Wood** **Pieces & Slate** M N W	**X** **Wood Pieces & Slate** TGPK pg. 105	**X** **Crayon Stroke** GSS pg. 69	**Y** **Wood Pieces & Slate** TGPK pg. 106	**Y** **Crayon Stroke** GSS pg. 70
27	**Z** **Wood Pieces & Slate** TGPK pg. 107	**Z** **Crayon Stroke** GSS pg. 71	**Review with Wood** **Pieces & Slate** X Y Z	**Activity Page** TGPK pg. 108 GSS pg. 72-73	**Activity Page** TGPK pg. 109 GSS pg. 74-75
Weeks to Follow	***Review Capitals** L F E H T I U	**Wood Pieces &** **Slate Activities**	**Review Capitals** C O Q G S J D P B R	*Rock, Rap, Tap &* *Learn* **CD**	**Review Capitals** K A V M N W X Y Z

FAQs

Should I ever have children trace their letters?
Our preschool program has a developmentally appropriate workbook that is just for tracing. Our printing and cursive workbooks have a large model for children to finger trace before they write. Tracing often is the precursor to forming letters independently. However, we discourage you from having a child trace dot-dot letters or shapes, because these are visually confusing and the child is going dot-dot-dot. If you want a child to trace, use a highlighter. It is important to watch children as they trace to ensure they don't trace a letter from the bottom up or in the wrong sequence. Model the letter, have the child trace over the letter, and then write the letter independently.

Why do children have difficulty forming their names with capital and lowercase letters?
Children have to learn 26 capitals, 26 lowercase letters, and 9 numbers. If they are bombarded with all the possibilities, that's when they struggle and begin to accommodate by drawing their letters. You are more likely to see reversals, bottom-up formation, mixing of capitals and lowercase letters. If you teach capital letters first, preschoolers will enter kindergarten with good habits. When lowercase letters are introduced, children will learn how to compare them to the capital letters and form them appropriately on the double line paper with the correct starting place, sequence, size, and placement. If you are eager for your preschoolers to learn their names in title case, we suggest direct demonstration until they have mastered the formations correctly. Please see page 26 and 27 of this guide for valuable advice on helping your students learn to write their names.

How do I help children transition from writing their names in block capital letters to lowercase letters?
Children in kindergarten will be ready to learn to write their names with lowercase letters. Once they can form all their capital letters starting from the top and with correct formation, they are ready to learn lowercase letters. These are harder because they have different starting places, different sizes, and are placed either above the line, within the lines or below the lines. Use the HWT name cards that show names in block capitals and title case. Demonstrate one letter at a time using the double line paper. Kindergarten teachers introducing lowercase will tell their students that they are big kids now and ready to learn lowercase letters. Children who have learned capitals first will have great habits and will master lowercase letters easily.

Where can I find more research on Handwriting Without Tears?
You can find all of the most current research at www.hwtears.com. Also, below is the reference to the research discussed on page 64 of this guide.

Research states that close to 50% of 3-year-olds are already using a mature tripod grasp.*
*Schneck, C.M., & Henderson , A. (1990). Descriptive analysis of the developmental progression of grip position for pencil and crayon in nondysfunctional children. *American Journal of Occupational Therapy, 44,* 893–900.
Tseng, M.H. (1998). Development of pencil grip position in preschool children. *Occupational Therapy Journal of Research, 18,* 207–224.
Weinraub, D.L. (1999). *The Effects of The Use of Broken Crayons Upon Grasp Development in Conjunction with Occupational Therapy.* Unpublished master's theses, Touro College, Far Rockaway, NY.
Yakimishyn, J.E. & Magill-Evans, J. (2002). Comparisons among tools, surface orientation, and pencil grasp for children 23 months of age. *American Journal of Occupational Therapy, 56,* 564–572.

If children tilt their papers, will it cause their writing to slant?
Beginner writers should keep their paper straight in front of them as they are learning to print letters and words. Children printing sentences should tilt their paper at a slight angle to follow the natural arc of their writing hand; this will not result in slanted letters.

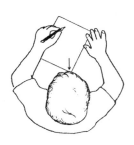
Left-Handed

Right-handed

© 2008 Handwriting Without Tears

Why do you teach children to write vertically as opposed to slanting their cursive handwriting?

We use a vertical style of print and cursive because it is easier to learn and read. The vertical stroke is developmentally easier. Occupational therapist Jan Olsen developed the program based on the developing skills of children to make handwriting a natural and automatic skill for all. If your child is a natural slanter, that's ok! However, forcing all children to slant to can lead to messy writing.

Students are required to write on the first day of school. Although the best practice may be to teach handwriting before the students actually have to write sentences and words, this is not possible with the demands put on teachers today. How should this be addressed?

Although research suggests that students benefit from explicit and supplemental instruction in forming and writing the letters of the alphabet, in some cases children are expected to write content before knowing how to write the letters. To give children the best experience for success, you would first teach them their letters and then have them transition to functional writing as they develop the ability to combine letters in words and words in sentences. As ideal as that sounds, we understand that there are several reasons beyond handwriting for exposing children to the writing process. As long as students are getting proper handwriting instruction, they can have writing exploration at any stage. You might not have the best writing results the first few months of school, but if you want to expose students to the process of writing, then exploration (i.e. free writing) is your only alternative. Students shouldn't write freely unless handwriting instruction is part of their everyday curriculum. The goal is to override any habits that might be formed during the exploratory phase. This will happen only if proper handwriting instruction is occurring daily.

Can more than one capital letter be taught in the same day?

Yes, more than one capital letter may be taught in the same day. You will want to teach from the similar group of letters and make sure that all students have mastered one letter before beginning the next.

Why does HWT use only capital letters in pre-k?

When children learn to write their names in pre-k, capitals are easier. However, they can still learn to recognize their names in title case (capital first, then lowercase). Learning to write is a part of a child's literacy development. Teachers must be careful not to confuse reading and writing when looking at a child's literacy development. Learning to read and write letters requires different skills. When learning to write their names, students should:

1. Start each letter correctly.
2. Use the correct steps in forming each letter.
3. Use the correct size.
4. Place the appropriately beside one another.

For capital letters, this easy! They all have:
- 1 starting place (at the top)
- 1 size (they are all the same size)
- 1 position (they all sit beside each other in the same way)

Lowercase are much more difficult. They can have:
- 4-5 different starting places
- 2 different sizes (full sized letters and half sized letters in relation to capital size)
- 3 different positions (ascending, descending, and letters that fit between the lines)

Do a demonstration for the directors and teachers from the schools you are consulting, and show them that capitals are easier than lowercase. Demonstrate capital **A B D P Q** and the lowercase **a b d p q.** You can also explain how the lowercase letters are more difficult to discriminate from one another and that the capital letters are easy.

Handwriting Without Tears®

A
Big line
Big line
Little line

B
Big line
Little curve
Little curve

C
Big C curve

D
Big line
Big curve

E
Big line
Little line
Little line
Little line

F
Big line
Little line
Little line

G
Big curve
Little line
Little line

H
Big line
Big line
Little line

I
Big line
Little line
Little line

J
Big line
Turn
Little line

K
Big line
Little line
Little line

L
Big line
Little line

M
Big line
Big line
Big line
Big line

N
Big line
Big line
Big line

O
Big C curve
Keep going

P
Big line
Little curve

Q
Big C curve
Keep going
Little line

R
Big line
Little line
Little line

S
Little curve
Turn
Little curve

T
Big line
Little line

U
Big line
Turn
Big line

V
Big line
Big line

W
Big line
Big line
Big line
Big line

X
Big line
Big line

Y
Little line
Big line

Z
Little line
Big line
Little line

www.hwtears.com